fresh and fabulous QUILTS

Cheryl Brown

Dedication

I lovingly dedicate this book to my amazing husband, Neil, who has given me my wings to fly, not to mention my sheep to count.

Acknowledgements

My heartfelt thanks go to:

My dear mother-in-law, Mary, for helping me along the road to loving quilts.

My quilting friends; especially all of my coworkers, past and present, at Threads of Time, whom I love dearly.

Jenny for starting me on this publishing journey!

My mom and dad, who gave me everything I ever needed to succeed. I love you two!

Fresh and Fabulous Quilts

© 2008 by Cheryl Brown

That Patchwork Place® is an imprint of Martingale & Company®.

Martingale & Company
20205 144th Ave. NE
Woodinville, WA 98072-8478 USA
www.martingale-pub.com

Credits

President & CEO ~ Tom Wierzbicki

Publisher ~ Jane Hamada

Editorial Director ~ Mary V. Green

Managing Editor ~ Tina Cook

Technical Editor ~ Nancy Mahoney

Copy Editor ~ Marcy Heffernan

Design Director ~ Stan Green

Production Manager ~ Regina Girard

Illustrator ~ Adrienne Smitke

Cover & Text Designer ~ Stan Green

Photographer ~ Brent Kane

Printed in China
13 12 11 10 09 08   8 7 6 5 4 3 2 1

Library of Congress Cataloging-in-Publication Data
Library of Congress Control Number: 2008027493

ISBN: 978-1-56477-823-9

MISSION STATEMENT
Dedicated to providing quality products and service to inspire creativity.

CONTENTS

Introduction ✳ 5

PROJECTS

Flower Power ✳ 7

Counting Sheep ✳ 17

Holly Jolly ✳ 27

In the Corner ✳ 39

L-O-V-E ✳ 43

Have a Heart ✳ 49

Every Blooming Thing ✳ 57

Fruit Basket ✳ 67

Quiltmaking Basics ✳ 71

About the Author ✳ 80

INTRODUCTION

Like many quilters, I remember playing under quilt frames as a child. There was a sense of magic when the neighbor ladies came to my mom's house to quilt while I played under the layers of fabric and batting. Many years later, my love for quilting increased as I learned to piece and quilt myself. Now I love every aspect of the art of quiltmaking. I love to design, to select fabric, to appliqué a block, to piece a top, and I love it when a quilt is quilted and bound.

In this book, I hope to share my love of both quilting and hand appliqué. I enjoy bright, colorful designs and not-too-hard appliqué. I take pleasure in the design and construction processes. I hope you enjoy the process of quiltmaking, too, and love the quilts you create. Let your imagination run wild; put your own twist on my designs. Use *your* favorite colors. In other words, have fun! After all, that's what quilting is all about!

Finished Quilt: 67½" x 87½"
Finished Blocks: 10" x 10"

FLOWER POWER

Feeling groovy? This appliqué quilt is simple, yet fun. It's a great way to use those fabulous '60s fabrics!
You may even find yourself saying, "Far out!"

Materials

Yardages are based on 42"-wide fabric.

2⅜ yards of floral fabric for Power block centers and outer border

⅔ yard *each* of 18 assorted bright prints for blocks

⅜ yard of hot pink fabric for inner border

¾ yard of bright striped fabric for binding

5⅝ yards of fabric for backing

72" x 92" piece of batting

Template plastic

Fine-point permanent pen

Cutting

All measurements include ¼"-wide seam allowances.

From *each* of the 18 assorted bright prints, cut:

2 rectangles, 3" x 15" (36 total)

4 rectangles, 3" x 10" (72 total)

2 rectangles, 3" x 6" (36 total)

From *each* of 17 of the 18 assorted bright prints, cut:

4 squares, 5⅞" x 5⅞" (68 total)

4 squares, 5½" x 5½" (68 total)

From the floral fabric, cut:

8 strips, 8" x 42"

3 strips, 4½" x 42"; crosscut into 18 squares, 4½" x 4½"

From the hot pink fabric, cut:

7 strips, 1½" x 42"

Flower Block Assembly

The Flower blocks are made in matching pairs. You'll need a 5⅞" and a 5½" square *each* from two contrasting prints. Refer to the photo on page 6 for color-placement ideas.

❶ Using pattern A on page 11, trace the flower shape onto the template plastic, making sure to include the center diagonal line. Cut out the flower shape, but do not cut along the diagonal line. (The diagonal line will be used later to center the template on the fabric squares.)

❷ Use a permanent pen to draw a diagonal line on the right side of each 5⅞" square as shown on the pattern. Then using template A and aligning the diagonal lines, make small (⅛") marks to indicate the flower center placement. (These lines will be in the seam allowance after the seam is sewn.)

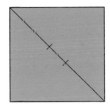

Mark diagonal line
and flower center.

❸ Use a permanent pen to draw a diagonal line on the right side of each 5½" square as shown on the pattern. Align template A on the drawn line and trace around the template with a pencil. Cut out the flower shape, leaving a scant ¼" seam allowance around the marked line. (The marked line will be your stitching line.)

Cut out flower.

❹ Place a flower shape on the contrasting background square from step 2, matching the center diagonal lines and placement marks. Hand appliqué the flower in place referring to "Appliqué" on page 73 for details as needed.

❺ Cut each flower square in half along the marked diagonal line to make two triangles. Sew two contrasting triangles together as shown, using a ¼" seam allowance, to make a 5½" square; press.

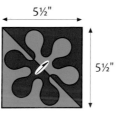

Make 2 matching (68 total).

❻ Repeat steps 2–5 to make 68 blocks total.

❼ Sew four blocks together as shown, so that the diagonal seams meet in the center. Make 17 Flower blocks.

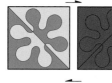

Make 17.

Power Block Assembly

To make the Power blocks you can either use the patterns provided to trim the pieces, or you can wing it, cutting each angle randomly, which makes each block a little bit different. For each block you'll use three fabrics: the floral fabric for the center, and two additional fabrics, which I call fabrics 1 and 2. The following directions use patterns B, C, and D on pages 12–14. If you choose to use the patterns provided, first make a template from them using the template plastic. (Be sure to enlarge pattern D.)

❶ Using template B and a floral square, trace and cut the block center.

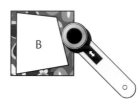

❷ Center and sew a 3"x 6" strip of fabric 1 to the top and bottom of the block center, leaving a tail on each end as shown. Trim the tails of the strips to match the angle of the block center.

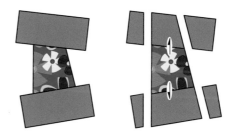

❸ Center and sew a 3" x 10" strip of fabric 1 to each side of the block as shown, again leaving a tail on each end. Use template C to trim the block.

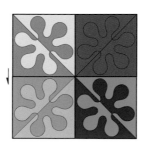

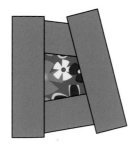

4 Center and sew a 3" x 10" strip of fabric 2 to opposite sides of the block. Trim the strips to match the angle on the block. Center and sew a 3" x 15" strip of the same fabric to the remaining sides of the block, leaving a tail on each end; press. Use template D or a square ruler to trim the block to 10½" square.

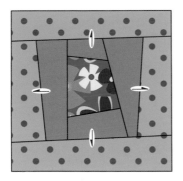

5 Repeat steps 1–4 to make 18 Power blocks total.

Quilt Top Assembly

1 Arrange the Flower blocks and Power blocks in seven rows of five blocks each as shown, alternating the appliquéd blocks and pieced blocks in each row and from row to row. Sew the blocks in each row together. Press the seam allowances toward the Power blocks. Sew the rows together. Press the seam allowances in one direction.

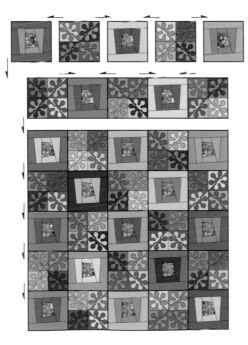

2 Sew the 1½"-wide hot pink strips together end to end to make one long strip. Refer to "Borders" on page 76 to measure, cut, and sew the strips to the sides and then the top and bottom of the quilt for the inner border.

3 Sew two 8"-wide floral strips together end to end to make a long strip. Make four long strips. Measure, cut, and sew the strips to the sides and then the top and bottom of the quilt for the outer border.

4 Use the scallop pattern on page 15 and the template plastic to make a scallop template. Trace the scallop template along the outer border of the quilt, making sure to align the valley between the scallops with the block seams as shown. The curved edge of the template should be aligned with the outer edge of the quilt.

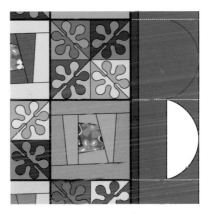

5 At each corner, mark a 45° angle using a marker that can be removed. (Don't use a permanent pen.) Trace the scallop template all the way to the end of the quilt side. At the corner, begin tracing the scallops along the adjacent side, overlapping the template as shown. Then realign the template, centering it on the diagonal line, and redraw the corner arc to smooth it out. Continue tracing in this way, repeating the centering process at each corner, until you have traced the scallop template all the way around the quilt. *Do not trim the scallops yet.* They will be cut after the quilting is finished.

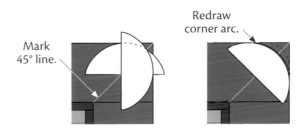

Mark 45° line.

Redraw corner arc.

Finishing the Quilt

❶ Referring to "Finishing the Quilt" on page 77, prepare the backing fabric. Layer the backing, batting, and quilt top; baste. After basting the layers together, hand or machine quilt as desired. (If you are taking your quilt to a long-arm quilter, you don't need to baste the layers together.)

❷ Cut the scallops along the marked lines. Referring to "Binding" on page 78, cut and prepare approximately 375" of 2¼"-wide bias binding. Sew the binding to the quilt.

BINDING ROUNDED EDGES

To sew the inside points, stop ¼" from the inside point with the needle in the down position, and then pivot the quilt, fitting the binding to the inside corner and along the next curve.

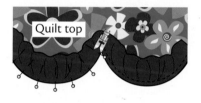

Continue sewing along each curve, pivoting at each inside point. Turn the binding to the back of the quilt, fitting it into each inside point. Hand stitch the binding in place as shown.

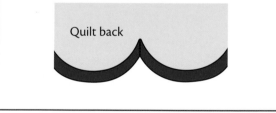

QUILTING SUGGESTION

I machine quilted an outline around the appliquéd flowers and used two different flower shapes and swirls in the Power blocks and outer border, filling the scallop shapes.

Appliqué pattern does not
include seam allowance.

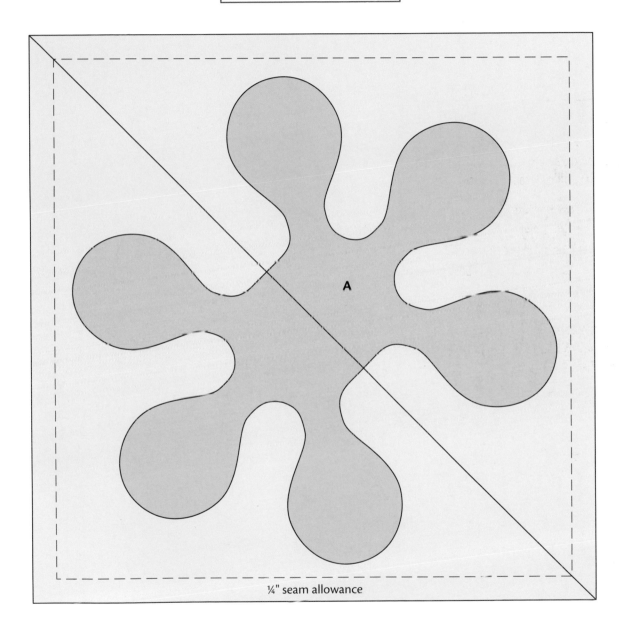

A

¼" seam allowance

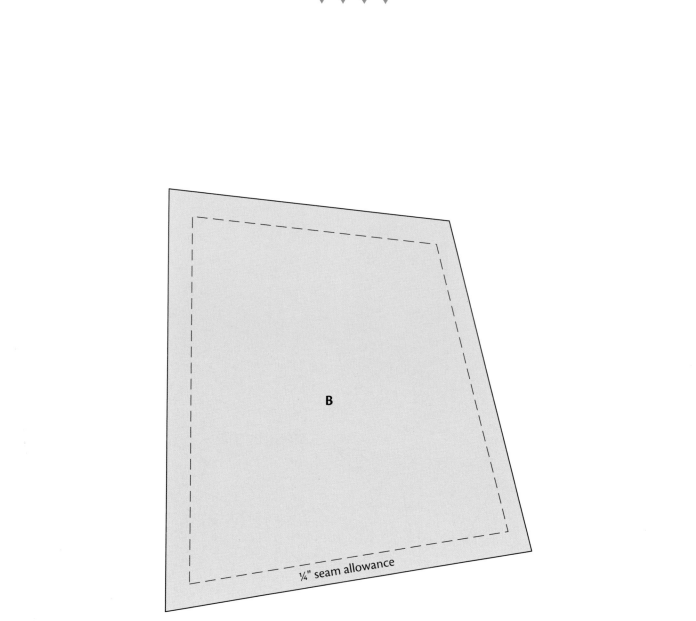

B

¼" seam allowance

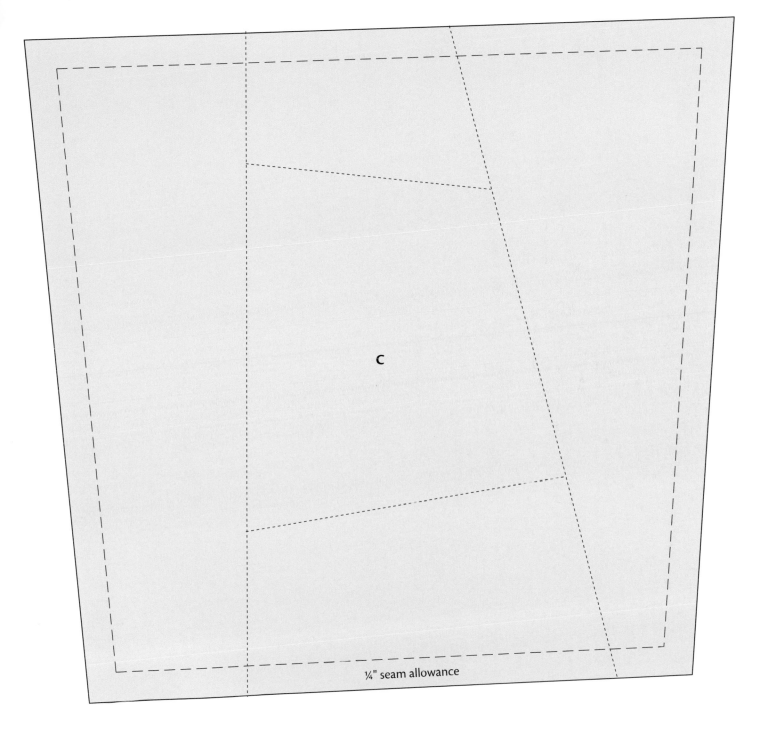

C

¼" seam allowance

Enlarge pattern 150%.

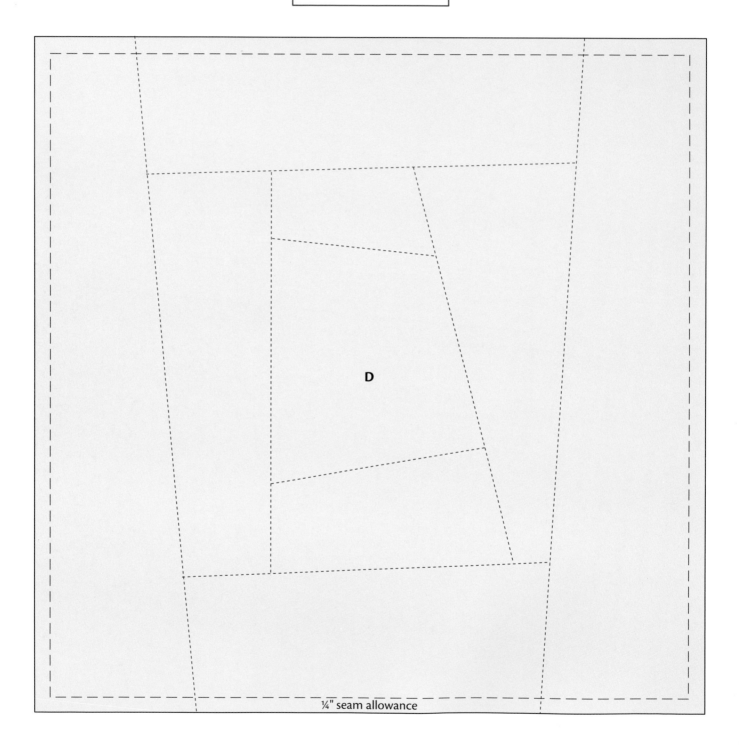

D

¼" seam allowance

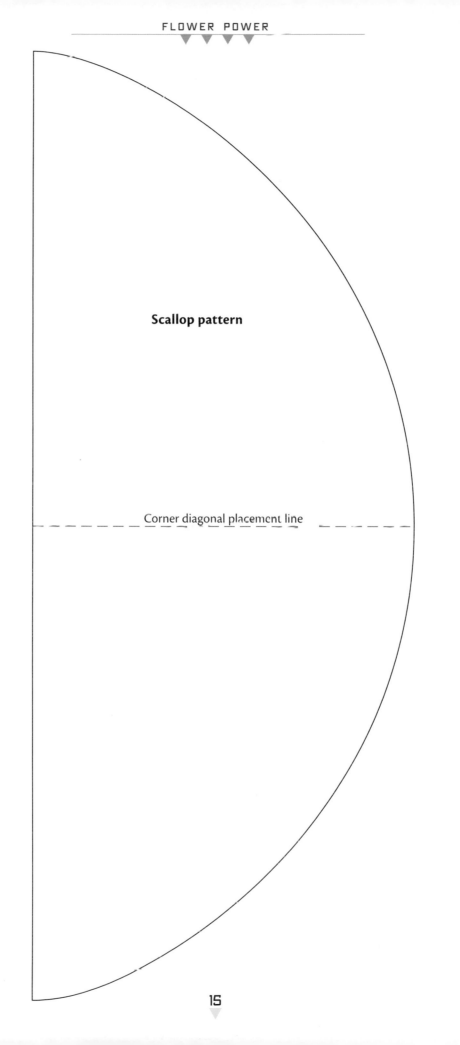

Scallop pattern

Corner diagonal placement line

Finished Quilt: 57" x 71"
Finished Blocks: 6" x 6"

COUNTING SHEEP

Can't sleep? Try counting sheep! These cute guys first came to life on my husband's sketch pad, and I told him I had to have them. Haven't we all felt like the poor little black sheep in the corner from time to time?

Materials

Yardages are based on 42"-wide fabric.

1⅜ yards of purple large sheep print for outer border

1¼ yards of black tone-on-tone fabric for sashing and sashing squares

1⅛ yards of purple-and-white print for block background and setting triangles

1⅛ yards of purple small sheep print for sashing and sashing squares

1 yard of black-and-white striped fabric for inner border and binding

⅝ yard *total* of assorted white fabrics for sheep and bed appliqués

¼ yard *total* of assorted cream fabrics for sheep appliqués

¼ yard *total* of assorted black fabrics for sheep and bed appliqués

⅓ yard of bright red fabric for bed appliqué

⅛ yard of bright green fabric for bed appliqué

3¾ yards of fabric for backing

61" x 75" piece of batting

Black embroidery floss for eyes

Freezer paper

Blue water-soluble pen

Cutting

All measurements include ¼"-wide seam allowances.

From the purple-and-white print, cut:

3 strips, 6½" x 42"; crosscut into 18 squares, 6½" x 6½"

3 squares, 9¾" x 9¾"; cut twice diagonally to yield 12 quarter-square triangles (You'll have two extra triangles.)

2 squares, 5⅛" x 5⅛"; cut once diagonally to yield 4 half-square triangles

From the purple small sheep print, cut:

10 strips, 2½" x 42"

6 strips, 1½" x 42"

From the black tone-on-tone fabric, cut:

20 strips, 1½" x 42"

3 strips, 2½" x 42"

From the black-and-white striped fabric, cut:

6 strips, 1½" x 42"

From the purple large sheep print, cut:

6 strips, 6½" x 42"

Appliquéing the Sheep Blocks

❶ Referring to "Appliqué" on page 73 and using the sheep patterns on pages 20–25, enlarge and trace each appliqué shape onto the dull side of the freezer paper, and cut out the templates.

❷ Using the assorted white fabrics for the sheep bodies, ears, and head tufts; the assorted cream fabrics for the sheep faces; and the assorted black fabrics for the sheep legs, press each freezer-paper template, shiny side down, onto the right side of the fabrics and trace around the template. The traced line will be the stitching line. Cut out each appliqué shape, leaving a scant ¼" seam allowance around the marked lines. Peel the freezer paper off of the fabric. Mark the eyes on each sheep head with a blue water-soluble pen. To keep the pieces for each sheep separate, store them in labeled plastic baggies until you're ready to lay them out. Using 15 of the 6½" purple squares and the pattern as a placement guide, hand appliqué a different sheep design in the center of each square. Be sure the purple squares are positioned on point. Appliqué the pieces in numerical order as indicated on each pattern.

❸ Referring to "Embroidery Stitches" on page 75 and using two strands of embroidery floss, straight stitch to outline each eye and satin stitch to fill in each eye.

Sashing and Sashing Square Assembly

❶ Sew a 1½"-wide black strip to each long side of a 2½"-wide purple strip to make strip set A. Press the seam allowances toward the black strips. Make eight strip sets. Crosscut the strip sets into 48 segments, 6½" wide.

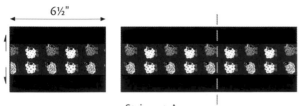

6½"

Strip set A.
Make 8. Cut 48 segments.

❷ Sew a 1½"-wide black strip to each long side of a 2½"-wide purple strip to make strip set B. Press the seam allowances toward the black strips. Make two strip sets. Crosscut the strip sets into 31 segments, 2½" wide.

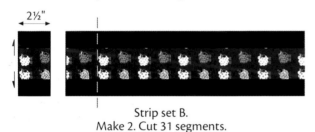

2½"

Strip set B.
Make 2. Cut 31 segments.

❸ Sew a 1½"-wide purple strip to each long side of a 2½"-wide black strip to make strip set C. Press the seam allowances toward the black strips. Make three strip sets. Crosscut the strip sets into 62 segments, 1½" wide.

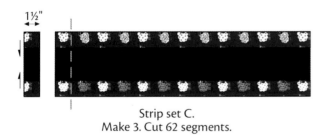

1½"

Strip set C.
Make 3. Cut 62 segments.

❹ Arrange two C segments and one B segment as shown. Sew the segments together to make a sashing square; press the seam allowances toward the center. Make 31 sashing squares.

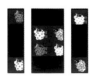

Make 31.

Quilt Top Assembly

❶ Arrange the appliquéd sheep blocks, the three remaining 6½" squares, the sashing units, the sashing squares, and the quarter-square and half-square triangles in diagonal rows as shown in the quilt assembly diagram below. Be sure to position the unappliquéd squares as shown with the jumping sheep in the top center position. You can arrange the remaining sheep blocks as desired.

❷ Sew the pieces together into diagonal rows. Press the seam allowances toward the sashing units. Sew the rows together, adding the corner triangles last; press.

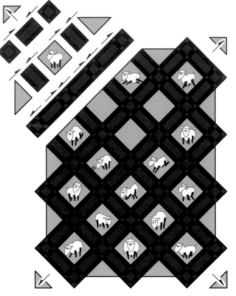

Quilt assembly

❸ To trim the sashing squares, align the ¼" mark on your ruler with the center of the block as shown. Use a rotary cutter to trim the excess block, leaving a ¼"-wide seam allowance. Square the corners of the quilt as necessary.

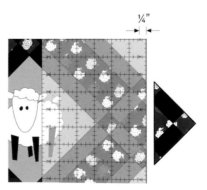

¼"

❹ Referring to "Appliqué" on page 73 and using the bed pattern on page 26, enlarge and trace each appliqué shape onto the dull side of the freezer paper and cut out the templates.

5 Using red for the bed frame, green for the bed quilt, white for the pillow and three thought dots, and black for the hair and one thought dot, press each freezer-paper template, shiny side down, onto the right side of the fabrics and trace. Cut out each appliqué shape, leaving a scant ¼" seam allowance around the traced line. Peel the freezer paper off of the fabric.

6 Referring to the photo on page 16 and the placement guide, position and hand appliqué the bed shapes in place. Appliqué the pieces in numerical order as indicated on the pattern.

Placement guide

Adding the Borders

1 Sew the 1½"-wide black-and-white strips together end to end to make one long strip. Refer to "Borders" on page 76 to measure, cut, and sew the strips to the top and bottom, and then the sides of the quilt for the inner border.

2 Sew the 6½"-wide purple sheep strips together end to end to make one long strip. Measure, cut, and sew the strips to the top and bottom, and then the sides of the quilt for the outer border.

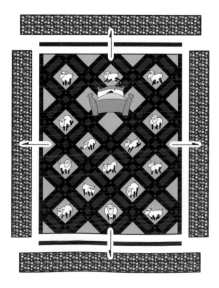

3 Referring again to "Appliqué" and using the black sheep pattern on page 25, enlarge and trace each appliqué shape onto the dull side of the freezer paper and cut out the templates.

4 Using black for the sheep body, head tuft, and legs, and using cream for the face and white for the ears, press each freezer paper template, shiny side down, onto the right side of the fabrics and trace. Cut out each appliqué shape, leaving a scant ¼" seam allowance around the traced line. Peel the freezer paper off of the fabric. Mark the eyes on the sheep head with a blue water-soluble pen. In the lower right-hand corner of the outer border as shown in the photo on page 16, hand appliqué the black sheep in place, appliquéing the pieces in the numerical order indicated on the pattern.

5 Referring to "Embroidery Stitches" on page 75 and using two strands of embroidery floss, straight stitch to outline each eye and satin stitch to fill in each eye.

Finishing the Quilt

1 Referring to "Finishing the Quilt" on page 77, prepare the backing fabric, and then layer the backing, batting, and quilt top; baste. After basting the layers together, hand or machine quilt as desired. (If you are taking your quilt to a long-arm quilter, you don't need to baste the layers together.)

2 Referring to "Binding" on page 78, cut and prepare approximately 270" of 2¼"-wide bias binding. Sew the binding to the quilt.

QUILTING SUGGESTION

I machine quilted around all the appliqué shapes, and echo quilted the sheep shape in the background squares. I quilted in the ditch along the sashing and sashing squares, quilted a wavy line through the middle of the sashing, and quilted a sheep motif in the outside border.

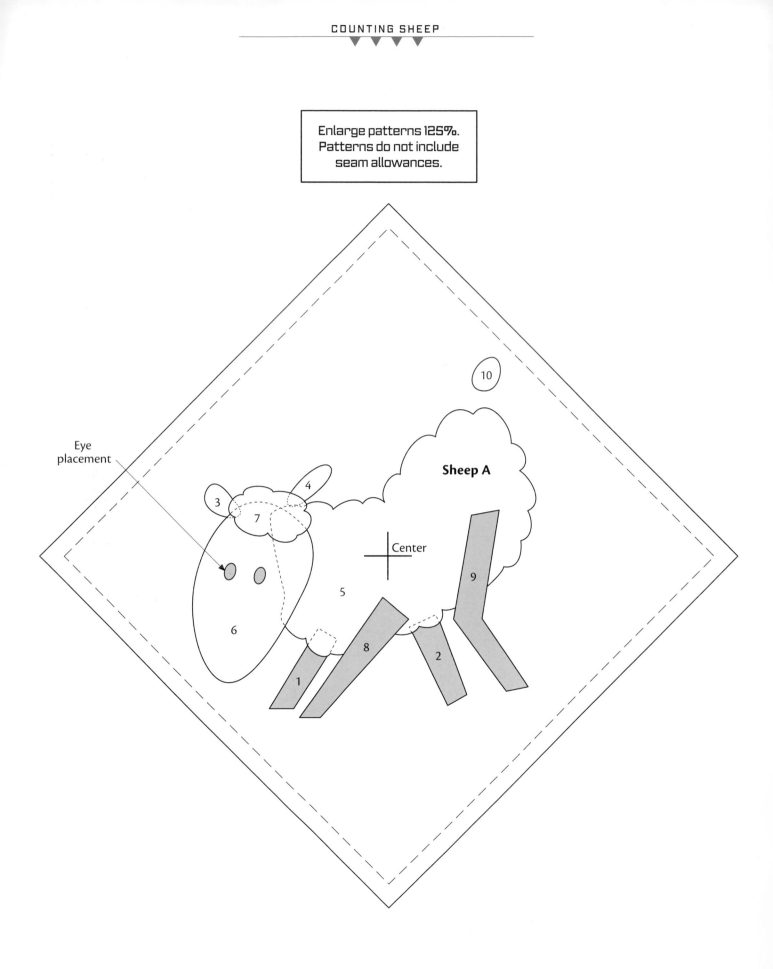

Enlarge patterns 125%.
Patterns do not include
seam allowances.

Eye placement

Sheep A

3

4

7

10

Center

9

5

6

8

2

1

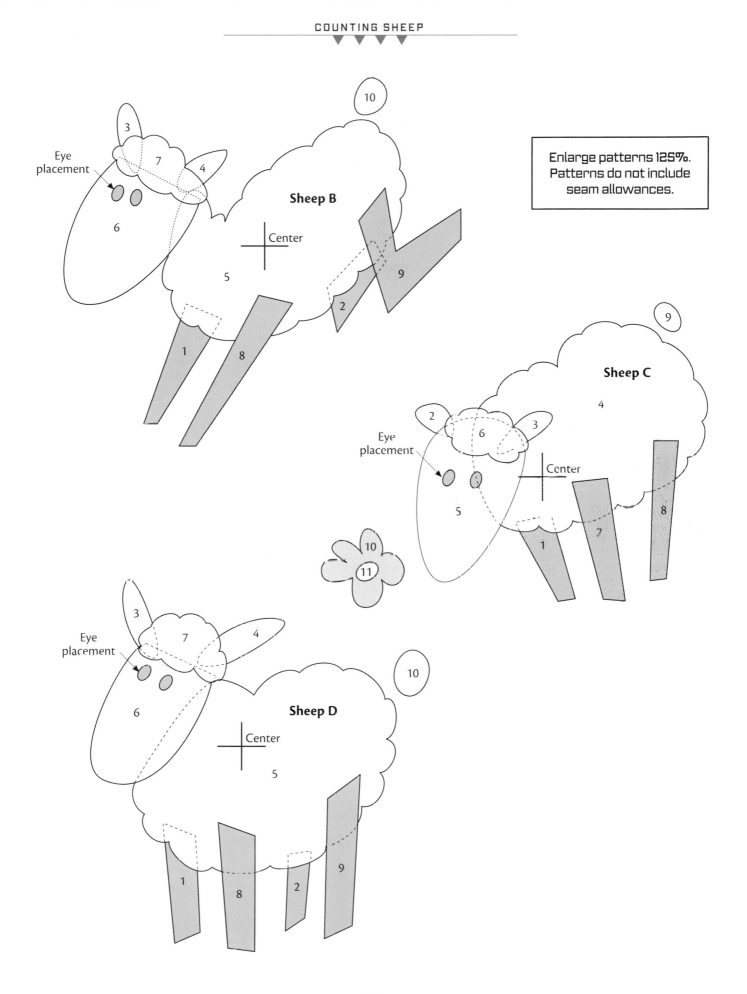

Enlarge patterns 125%.
Patterns do not include
seam allowances.

Sheep B

Eye placement

Sheep C

Eye placement

Sheep D

Eye placement

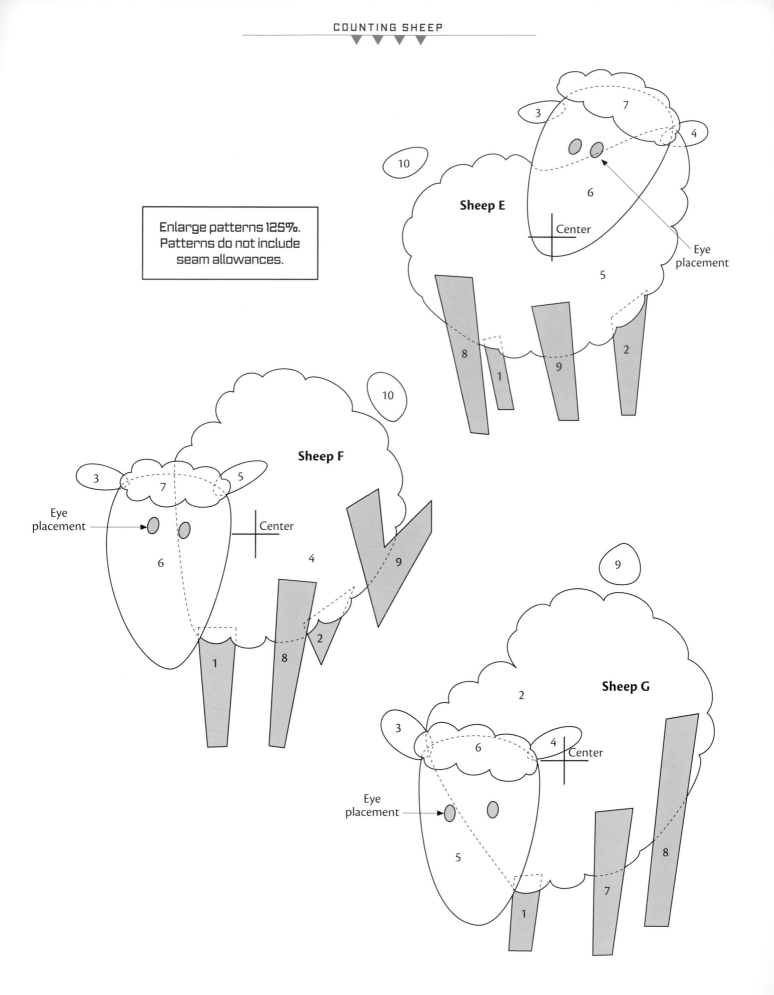

Enlarge patterns 125%.
Patterns do not include
seam allowances.

Sheep E

Center

Eye
placement

Sheep F

Center

Eye
placement

Sheep G

Center

Eye
placement

Enlarge patterns 125%.
Patterns do not include
seam allowances.

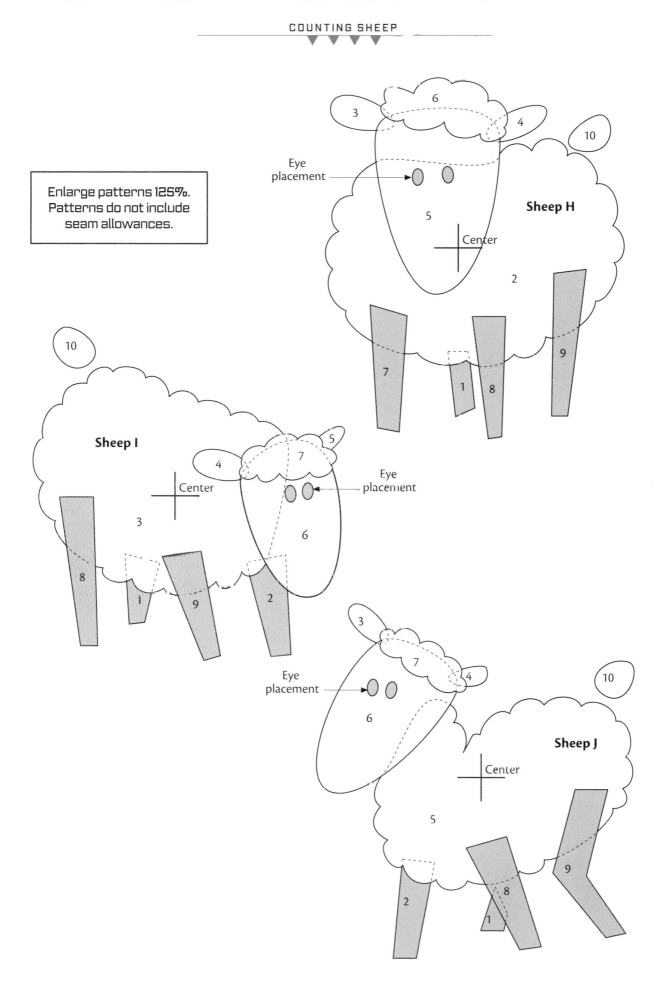

Eye
placement

Sheep H

Center

6
3
4
10
5
2
7
1
8
9

Sheep I

10

Center

5
4
7
Eye
placement

3
6
8
1
9
2

Sheep J

3
7
4
10
Eye
placement
6
Center
5
2
8
1
9

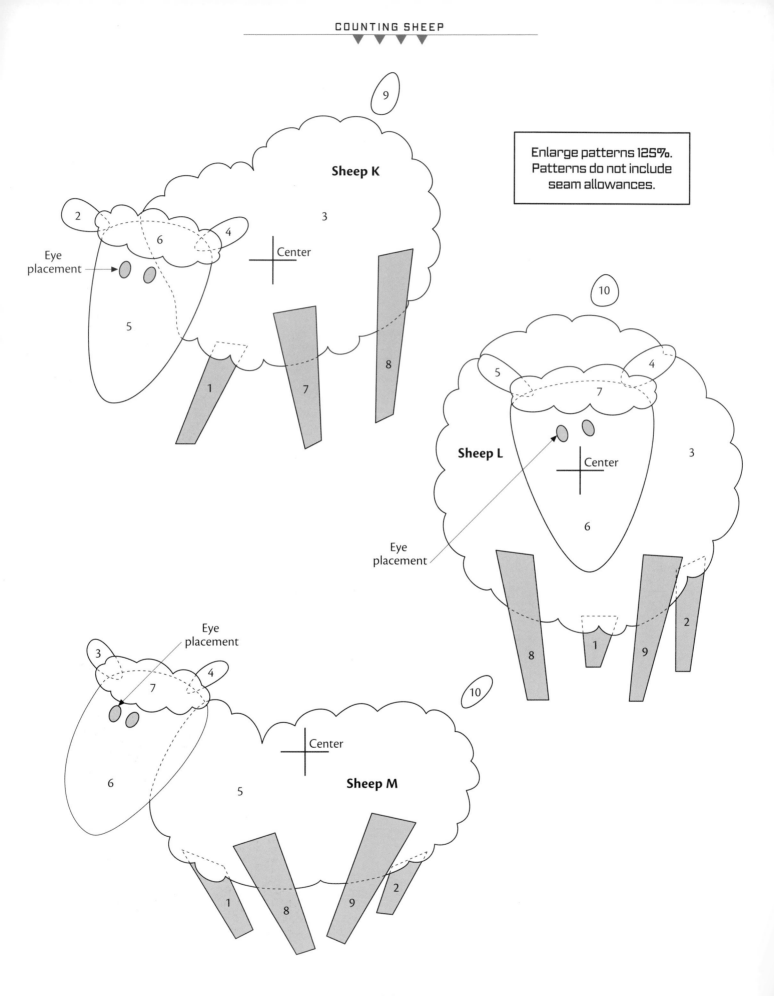

Enlarge patterns 125%.
Patterns do not include
seam allowances.

Sheep K

Eye placement

Center

Sheep L

Eye placement

Center

Eye placement

Sheep M

Center

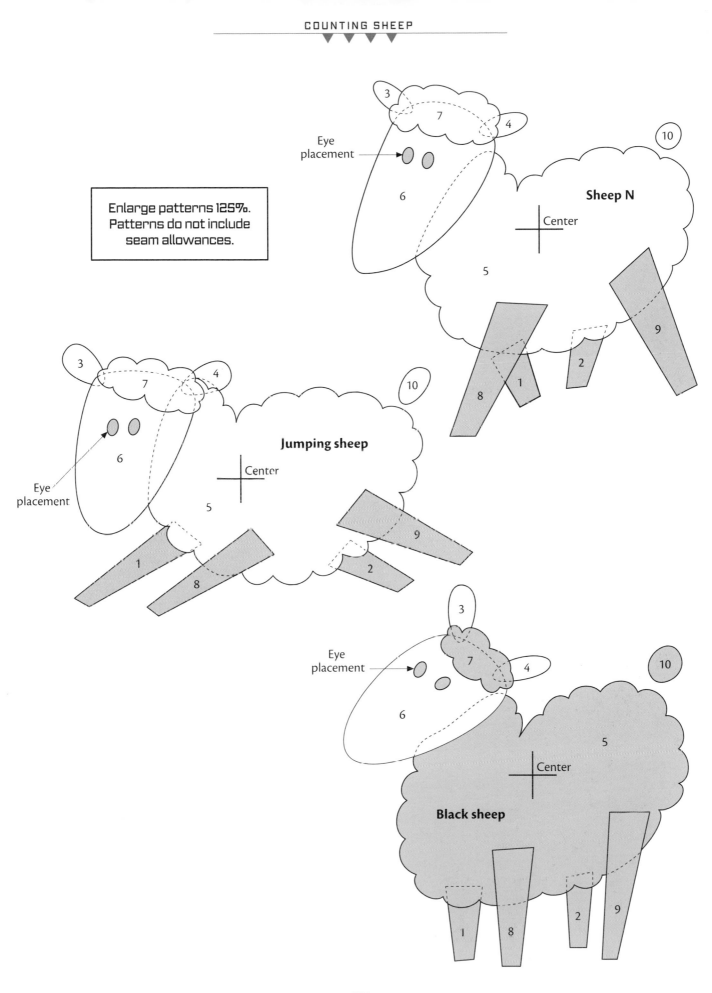

Enlarge patterns 125%.
Patterns do not include
seam allowances.

Eye placement

Sheep N

Center

3 7 4

6

5

10

9

2

1

8

3 7 4

6

Eye placement

Jumping sheep

Center

5

10

9

2

1

8

Eye placement

3

7 4

6

5

10

Center

Black sheep

1 8 2 9

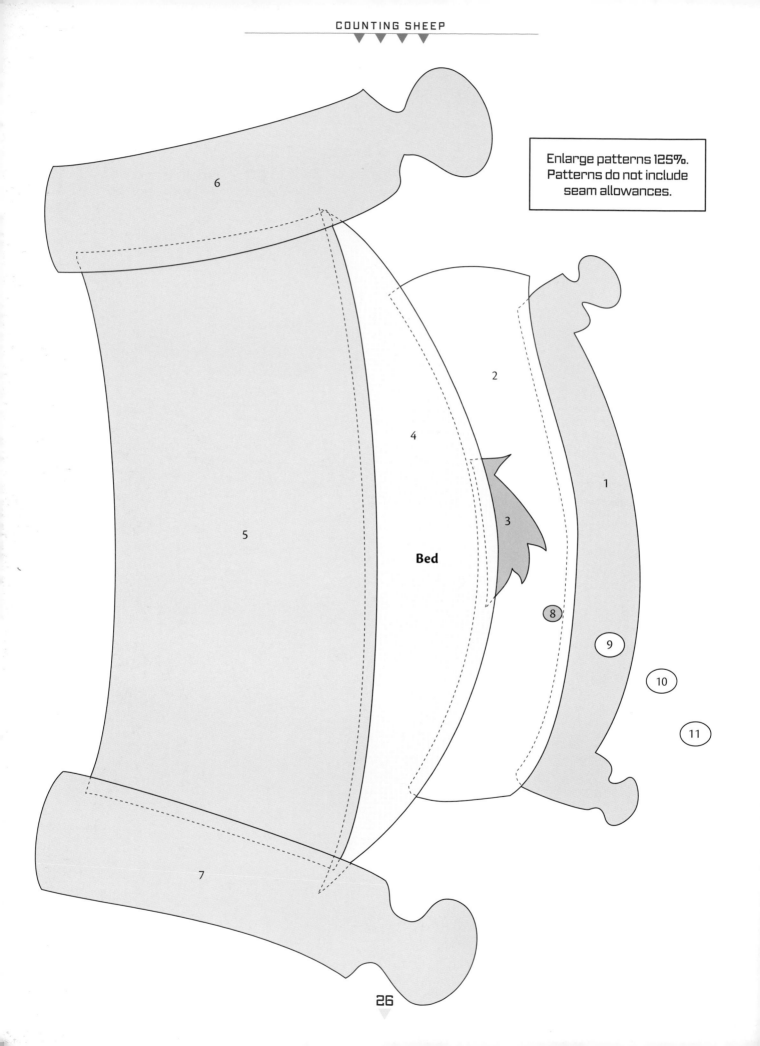

Enlarge patterns 125%.
Patterns do not include seam allowances.

HOLLY JOLLY

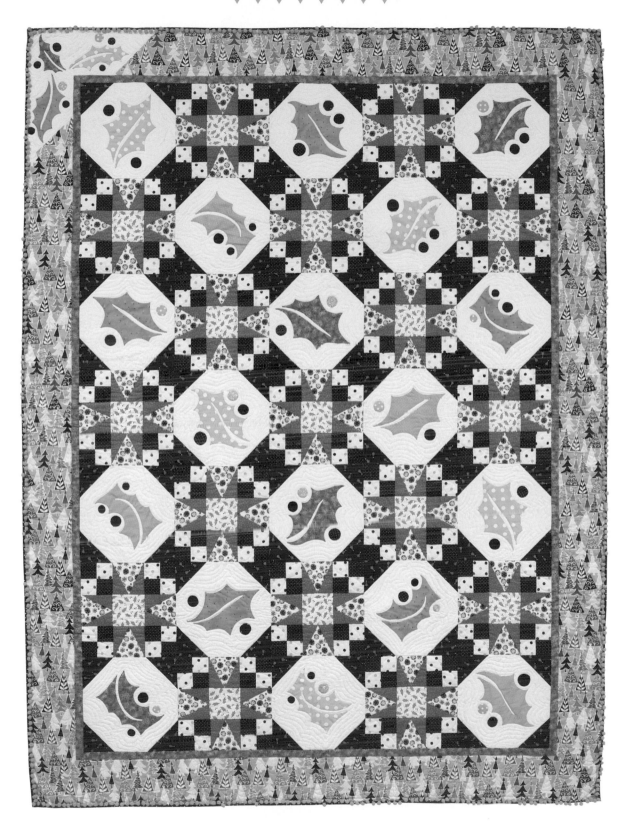

Finished Quilt: 74½" x 98½"
Finished Blocks: 12" x 12"

HOLLY JOLLY

Have a Holly Jolly Christmas! This quilt, with its splash of holly leaves, is a Yuletide greeting in itself.

Materials

Yardages are based on 42"-wide fabric.

3⅞ yards of tree print for outer border

2½ yards of white tone-on-tone fabric for Snowball blocks and outer border

1¾ yards of red-with-white-dot fabric for Star blocks and binding

1⅓ yards of red fabric for Snowball blocks

1 yard of dark green print for Star blocks

¾ yard of green-and-red print for Star blocks

¾ yard of white-with-small-dot fabric for Star blocks

½ yard of white-and-green print for Star block centers

½ yard of green tone-on-tone fabric for inner border

2¼ yards *total* assorted bright green prints for appliqués

½ yard *total* assorted bright red prints and assorted pink prints for appliqués

6⅜ yards of fabric for backing

79" x 103" piece of batting

10 yards of green pom-pom trim

Freezer paper

Template plastic

Cutting

All measurements include ¼"-wide seam allowances.

From the white tone-on-tone fabric, cut:
6 strips, 12½" x 42"; crosscut into 18 squares,
    12½" x 12½"
2 pieces, 6½" x 17"

From the red fabric, cut:
9 strips, 4½" x 42"; crosscut into 72 squares, 4½" x 4½"

From the green-and-red print, cut:
5 strips, 4½" x 42" strips

From the dark green print, cut:
7 strips, 4½" x 42"

From the red-with-white-dot fabric, cut:
9 strips, 2½" x 42"

From the white-with-small-dot fabric, cut:
9 strips, 2½" x 42"

From the white-and-green print, cut:
3 strips, 4½" x 42"; crosscut into 17 squares, 4½" x 4½"

From the green tone-on-tone fabric, cut:
8 strips, 1½" x 42"

From the tree print, cut:
2 strips, 6½" x 98½", from the *lengthwise* grain
4 strips, 6½" x 42", from the *crosswise* grain

Snowball Block Assembly

1 Using a pencil and a ruler, draw a diagonal line from corner to corner on the wrong side of each red square. Place marked squares on the corners of each white square as shown, right sides together. Sew on the marked line. Trim ¼" from the stitching line. Press the seam allowances toward the red corners. Make 18 Snowball blocks, each measuring 12½" square.

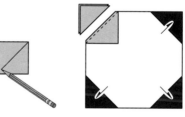

Make 18.

2 Referring to "Appliqué" on page 73 and using the holly patterns on pages 33–37, trace each appliqué shape onto the dull side of the freezer paper; cut out the freezer-paper templates. Make the quantity specified on the pattern for each shape.

3 Using the green fabrics for the holly leaves and the red and pink fabrics for the berries, press each freezer-paper template, shiny side down, onto the right side of the fabric and trace. Cut out each appliqué shape, leaving a scant ¼" seam allowance around the traced line. (The traced line will be the stitching line.) Set holly D, E, and F pieces aside until you are ready to appliqué them to the outer border.

④ Referring to the photo on page 27 for color-placement ideas, position each holly design in the center of a Snowball block and hand appliqué in place. Make 18 blocks.

Star Block Assembly

Patterns for pieces A and B appear on page 32.

① Referring to "Rotary Cutting Template Shapes" on page 72, make plastic templates for pieces A and B. From the green-and-red strips, cut 68 pieces using template A and your rotary-cutting tools. From the dark green strips cut 68 pieces using template B, and 68 pieces using template B reversed.

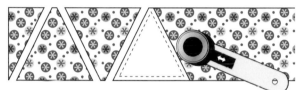

Cut 68.

Cut 68 and 68 reversed.

② Sew two B pieces (one regular and one reversed) to adjacent sides of one A piece as shown to make a star-point unit; press. Make 68 units.

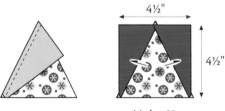

4½"

4½"

Make 68.

③ Sew a 2½"-wide white strip to the long side of a 2½"-wide red strip to make a strip set. Make nine strip sets. Crosscut the strip sets into 136 segments, 2½" wide.

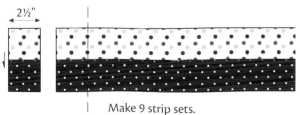

2½"

Make 9 strip sets.
Cut 136 segments.

④ Sew two segments together as shown to make a four-patch unit. Make 68 units.

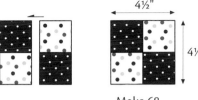

4½"

4½"

Make 68.

⑤ Sew four four-patch units from step 4, four star-point units from step 2 and one white-and-green square in rows as shown; press. Sew the rows together; press. Make 17 Star blocks, each measuring 12½" square.

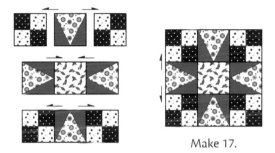

Make 17.

Quilt Top Assembly

① Arrange the blocks in seven rows of five blocks each, alternating the Snowball blocks and the Star blocks in each row and from row to row as shown in the quilt assembly diagram below.

② Sew the blocks in each row together; press the seam allowances toward the Snowball blocks. Sew the rows together; press the seam allowances in one direction.

Quilt assembly

29

3 Sew the 1½"-wide green strips together end to end to make one long strip. Refer to "Borders" on page 76 to measure, cut, and sew the strips to the top and bottom, and then the sides of the quilt for the inner border. The quilt should measure 62½" x 86½".

4 Sew two 42"-long tree print strips together end to end. Make two long strips and trim to measure 74½" long.

5 To make the left-side border, place a 6½" x 17" white piece on top of one 98½"-long tree print strip as shown, right sides together. Draw a line from the corner of the white piece to the corner of the border strip. Sew on the marked line. Trim ¼" from the stitching line and press the seam allowances toward the darker fabric. Starting from the white end of the strip, measure to 98½". Trim the excess fabric from the tree print end.

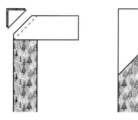

6 To make the top border, place the remaining 6½" x 17" white piece on top of a 74½"-long tree print strip as shown, right sides together. Draw a line from the corner of the white piece to the corner of the tree print strip. Sew on the marked line. Trim ¼" from the stitching line and press the seam allowances toward the darker fabric. Starting from the white end of the strip, measure to 74½". Trim the excess fabric from the tree print end.

7 Mark the centers of the quilt edges and border strips with pins. Measure the length and width of the quilt through the center in both directions. Place a pin at each end of the side border strips to indicate the length of the quilt. Repeat with the top and bottom border strips.

8 Pin the outer-border strip from step 5 to the left side of the quilt and the remaining 98½"-long outer-border strip to the right side of the quilt, matching the pin marks at the centers and matching the pins at the ends

of the border strips with the edges of the quilt. Stitch, beginning and ending the stitching ¼" from the raw edges of the quilt.

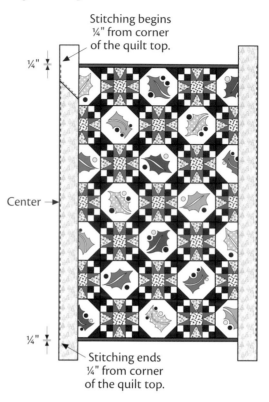

9 Repeat step 8 to pin and then sew the 74½"-long outer-border strip from step 6 to the top of the quilt and the remaining outer-border strip to the bottom of the quilt.

10 Fold the quilt diagonally, right sides together, and line up the edges of the border strips. Using a pencil and a ruler with a 45° angle printed on it, mark a 45° angle on the wrong side of each border strip, using your stitching line as a guide and starting at the intersection of the seam lines as shown.

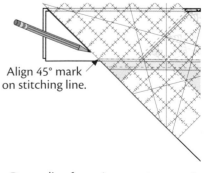

Align 45° mark on stitching line.

Draw a line from the seam intersection to outer edge of borders.

⑪ Pin carefully, matching the marked lines. Sew on the marked line. Backstitch at both ends. Trim the seam allowances to ¼" and press open. Miter the remaining corners in the same manner.

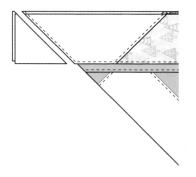

⑫ Using holly pieces D, E, and F, from step 3 of "Snowball Block Assembly" and the placement diagram on page 37, hand appliqué the pieces in the upper-left corner of the outer border.

Finishing the Quilt

① Referring to "Finishing the Quilt" on page 77, prepare the backing fabric, and then layer the backing, batting, and quilt top; baste. After basting the layers together, hand or machine quilt as desired. (If you are taking your quilt to a long-arm quilter, you don't need to baste the layers together.)

② Sew the pom-pom trim to the edge of the quilt using a scant ¼" seam allowance and a long basting stitch.

③ Referring to "Binding" on page 78, cut and prepare approximately 360" of 2¼"-wide bias binding. Sew the binding to the quilt.

QUILTING SUGGESTION

I machine quilted around each holly design and echo quilted the design in the Snowball blocks. For the Star blocks, I quilted around each star and used a continuous-line design in each block. I quilted Christmas trees in the borders.

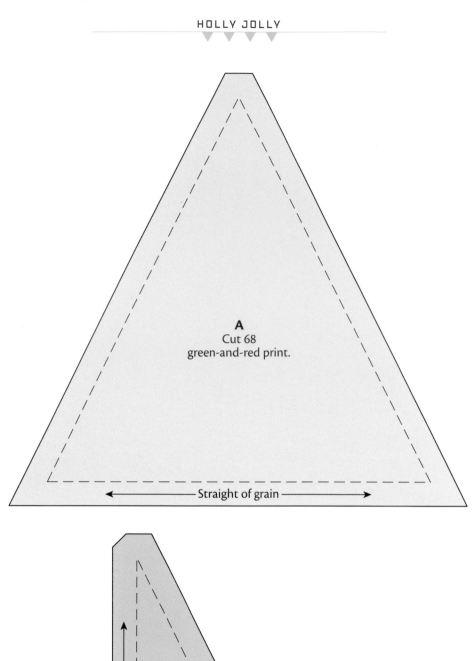

A
Cut 68
green-and-red print.

Straight of grain

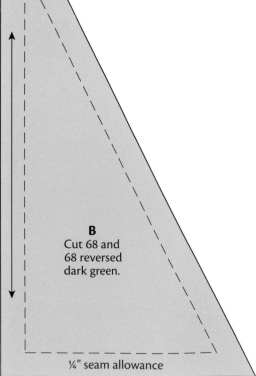

B
Cut 68 and
68 reversed
dark green.

¼" seam allowance

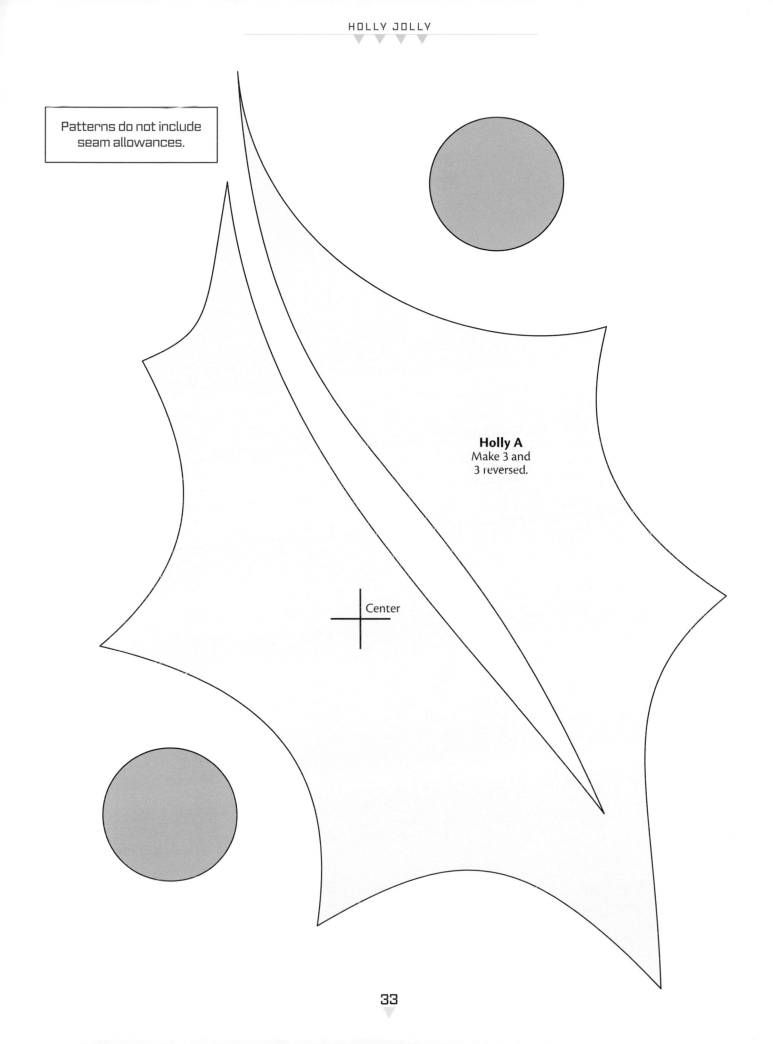

Patterns do not include seam allowances.

Holly A
Make 3 and
3 reversed.

Center

Patterns do not include
seam allowances.

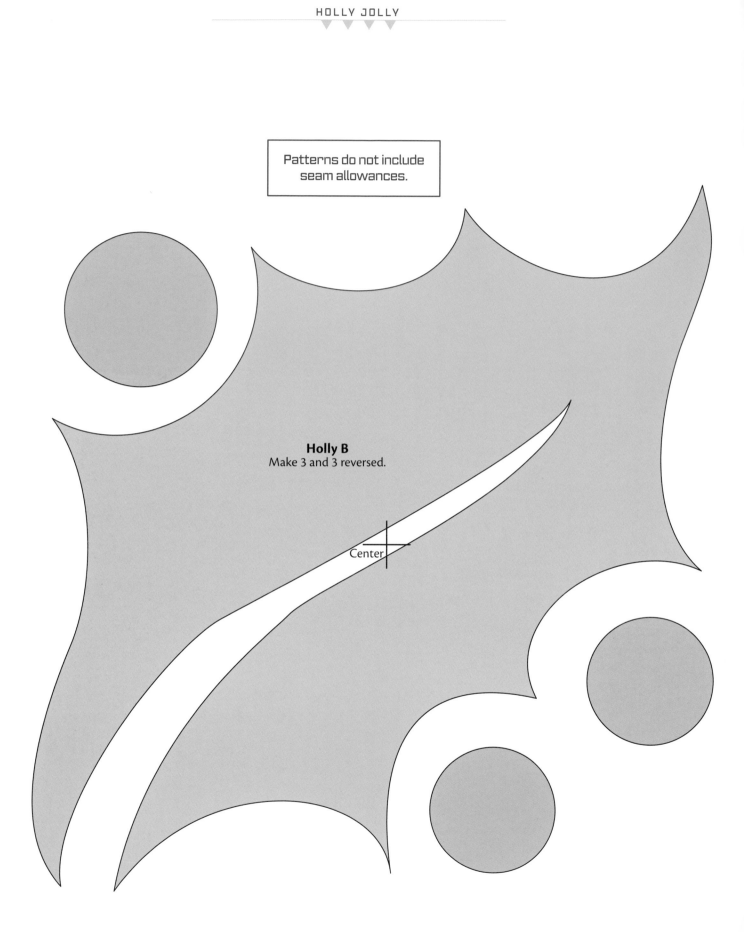

Holly B
Make 3 and 3 reversed.

Center

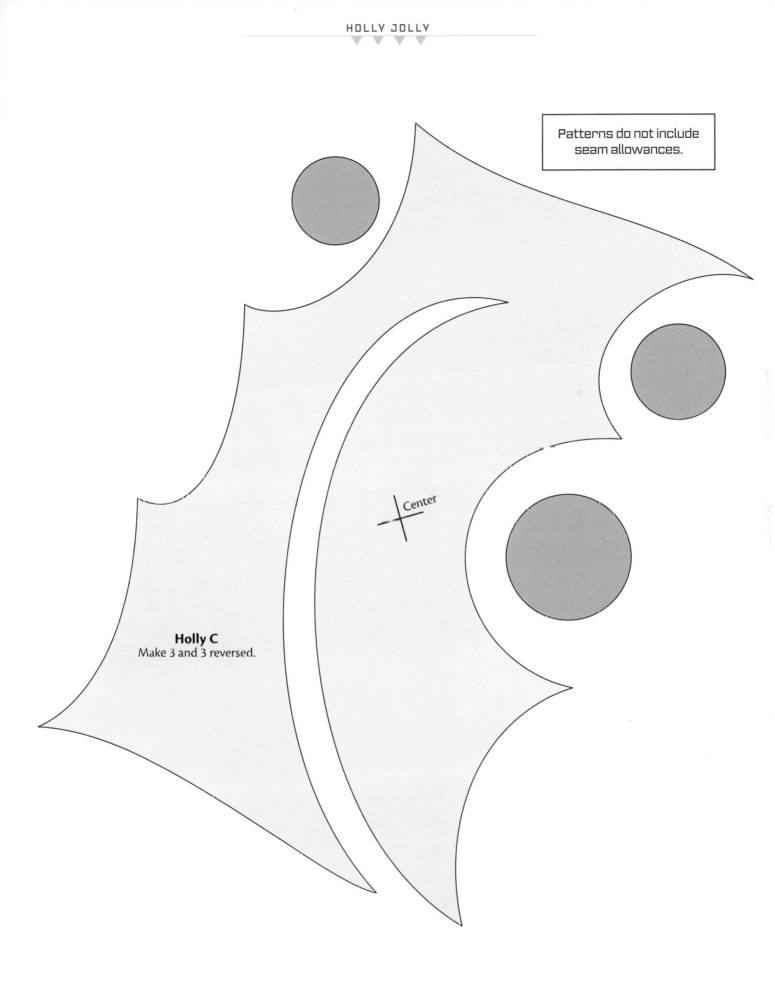

Patterns do not include seam allowances.

Center

Holly C
Make 3 and 3 reversed.

Patterns do not include
seam allowances.

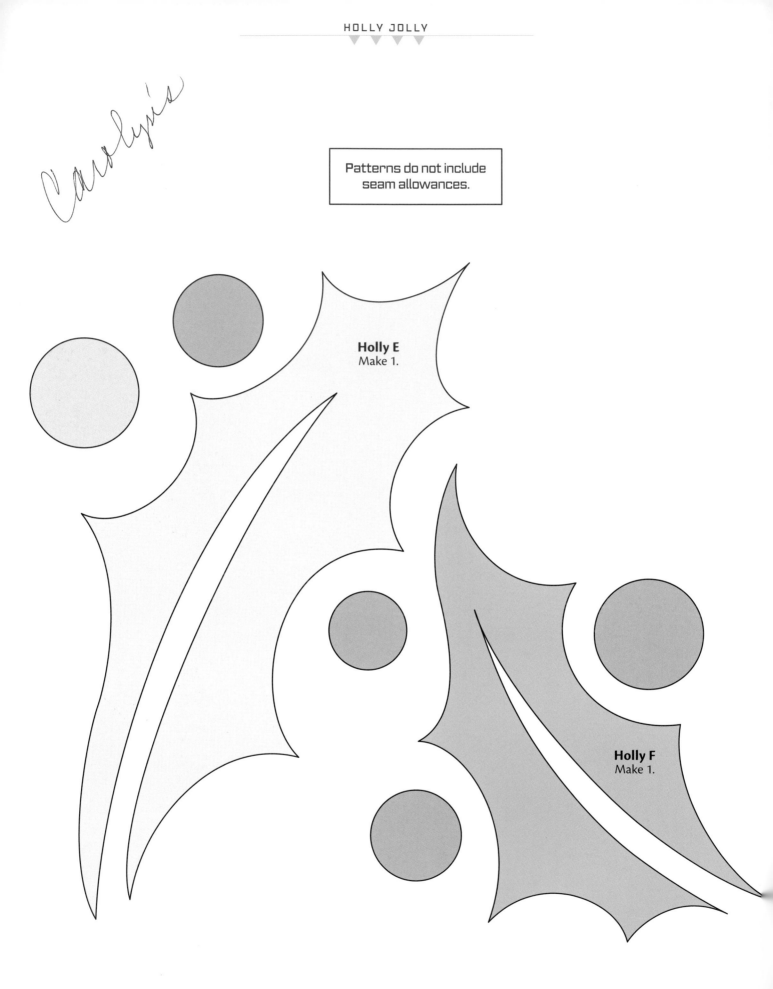

Holly E
Make 1.

Holly F
Make 1.

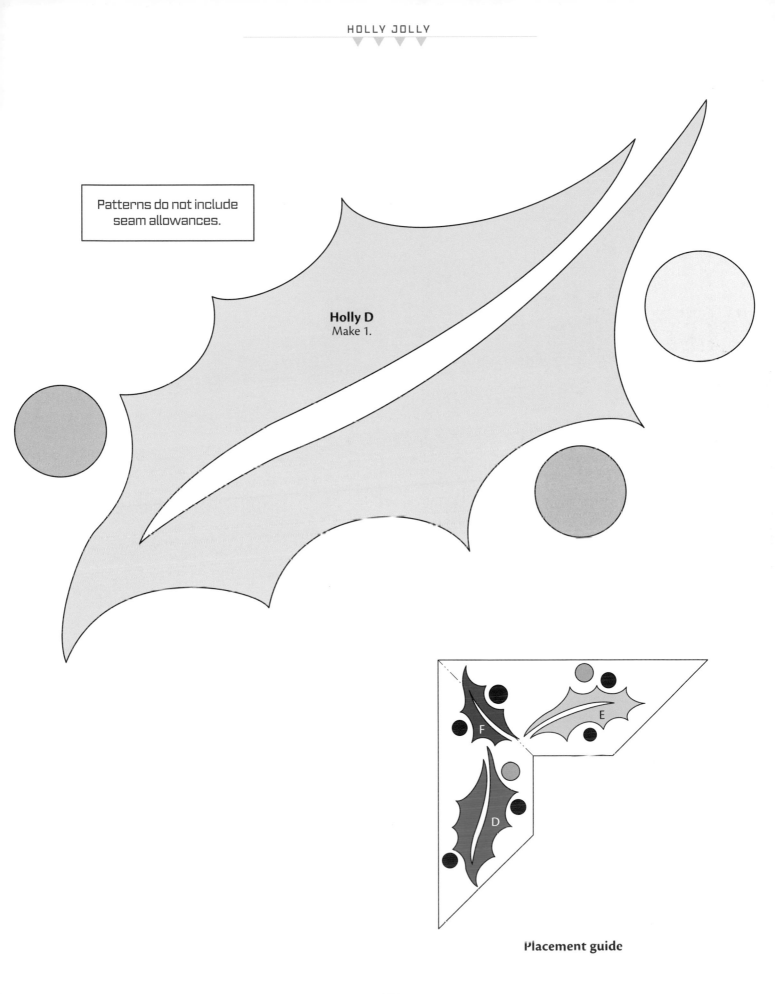

Patterns do not include seam allowances.

Holly D
Make 1.

Placement guide

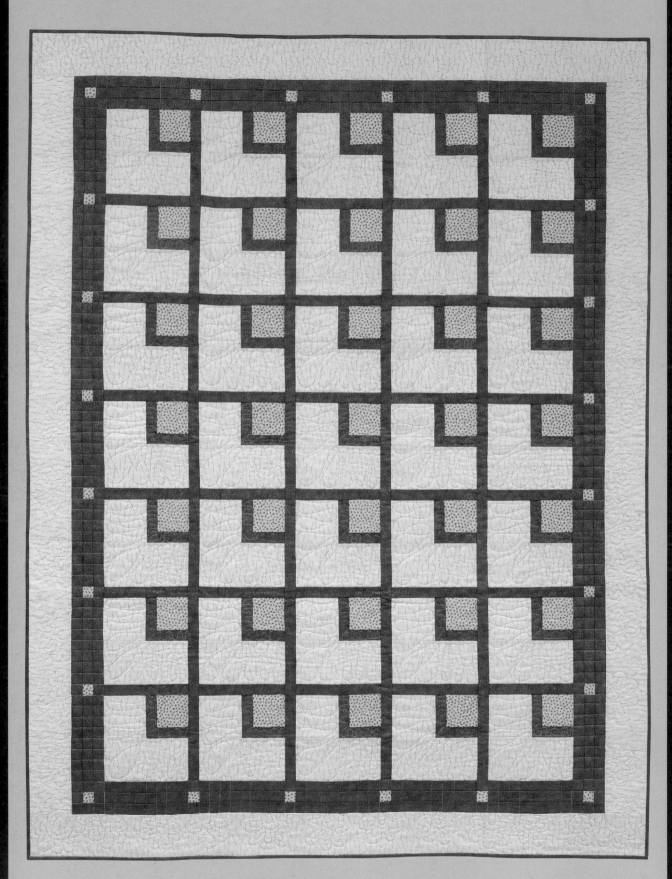

Finished Quilt: 58½" x 76½"
Finished Blocks: 8" x 8"

IN THE CORNER

Bright green and periwinkle—I love these colors together. The little square looks like a little postage stamp in the corner, hence the name. This quilt can easily be customized with your own three-fabric combination, and it's easy to make, too! Get out of your own little corner and make this one!

Materials

Yardages are based on 42"-wide fabric.

3 yards of green tone-on-tone fabric for blocks and outer border

2⅝ yards of periwinkle fabric for sashing, inner borders and binding

⅝ yard of lime green print for blocks and border squares

5 yards of fabric for backing

63" x 81" piece of batting

Cutting

All measurements include ¼"-wide seam allowances.

From the lime green print, cut:
4 strips, 3½" x 42"; crosscut into 35 squares, 3½" x 3½"
1 strip, 1½" x 42"; crosscut into 24 squares, 1½" x 1½"

From the periwinkle fabric, cut:
43 strips, 1½" x 42"; crosscut 25 *of the strips* into:
    8 rectangles, 1½" x 9½"
    56 rectangles, 1½" x 8½"
    35 rectangles, 1½" x 4½"
    35 rectangles, 1½" x 3½"

From the green tone-on-tone fabric, cut:
21 strips, 4½" x 42"; crosscut 14 *of the strips* into:
    35 rectangles, 4½" x 8½"
    35 squares, 4½" x 4½"

Block Assembly

1 Sew a 1½" x 3½" periwinkle rectangle to the left side of each 3½" lime green square; press. Sew a 1½" x 4½" periwinkle rectangle to the bottom of each unit; press.

2 Sew a 4½" green square to the left side of each unit; press. Then sew a 4½" x 8½" green rectangle to the bottom as shown; press. Make 35 blocks.

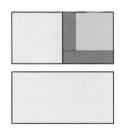
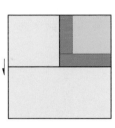

Make 35.

Quilt Top Assembly

1 Sew a 1½" x 8½" periwinkle rectangle to the top of each block; then sew a periwinkle rectangle to the bottom of five blocks as shown. Press seam allowances toward the periwinkle rectangles.

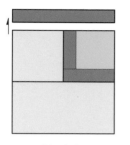

Block A.
Make 30.

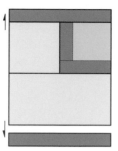

Block B.
Make 5.

2 Sew six A blocks together to make a vertical row as shown. Sew a B block to the bottom of the vertical row; press. Make five vertical rows. Each vertical row should measure 8½" x 64½".

3 Sew two 1½" x 42" periwinkle strips together end to end to make a sashing strip. Make six. Trim the sashing strips to measure 64½" long.

4 Sew a sashing strip to the left side of each vertical row; then sew a sashing strip to the right side of one row.

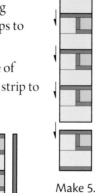

Make 5.

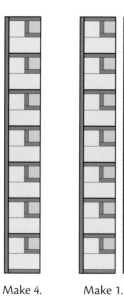

Make 4.   Make 1.

5 Referring to the quilt assembly diagram on page 41 and the "Helpful Hint" at right, sew the vertical rows together. The row with a sashing strip on each side should be on the right-hand side of the quilt. Press the seam allowances toward the sashing strips.

> ### HELPFUL HINT
>
> When the vertical block rows and long sashing strips are sewn together, it's important for the short horizontal sashing strips to correctly line up on each side of the long sashing strip. I've found an easy way to mark the long strips is to simply clip the long sashing strip to show the junctions that must match. Be sure to clip only halfway (⅛") into the seam allowance. Press the seam allowance toward the long sashing strip.
>
>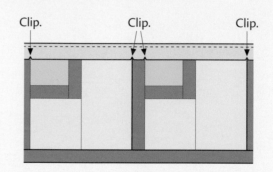
>
> Then sew the rows together, matching the seam junctions with the clips in the long sashing strip.
>
>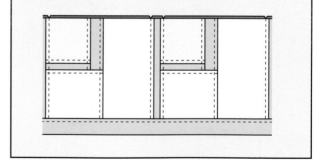

Adding the Borders

1 For each side border, sew two 1½" x 9½" periwinkle rectangles, five 1½" x 8½" periwinkle rectangles, and six 1½" green squares together as shown; press. Make two.

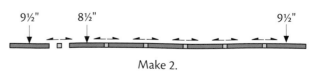

9½"   8½"   9½"

Make 2.

2 For the top and bottom borders, sew six 1½" green squares, two 1½" x 9½" periwinkle rectangles, and three 1½" x 8½" periwinkle rectangles together as shown; press. Make two.

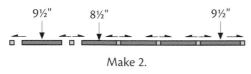

9½"   8½"   9½"

Make 2.

3 Sew the side border strips and then the top and bottom border strips to the quilt.

4 Sew the remaining six 1½"-wide periwinkle strips together end to end to make one long strip. Refer to "Borders" on page 76 to measure, cut, and sew the strips to the sides and then the top and bottom of the quilt for the inner border.

5 Sew the seven 4½"-wide green strips together end to end to make one long strip. Measure, cut, and sew the strips to the sides and then the top and bottom of the quilt for the outer border.

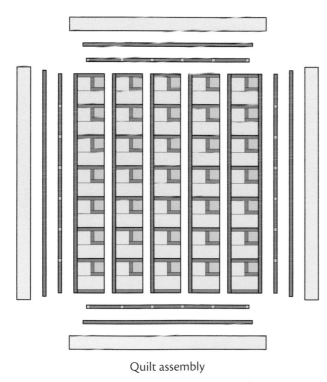

Quilt assembly

Finishing the Quilt

1 Referring to "Finishing the Quilt" on page 77, prepare the backing fabric, and then layer the backing, batting, and quilt top; baste. After basting the layers together, hand or machine quilt as desired. (If you are taking your quilt to a long-arm quilter, you don't need to baste the layers together.)

2 Referring to "Binding" on page 78, cut and prepare approximately 280" of 2¼"-wide bias binding. Sew the binding to the quilt.

QUILTING SUGGESTION
I machine quilted a blossom design in the outer border, which I then enlarged and quilted in the blocks. I quilted straight lines across the periwinkle borders.

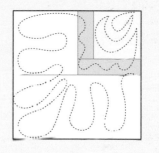

Finished Quilt: 29" x 21"

L–O–V–E

Everybody likes to fall—in love, that is. Your whole world just seems a little brighter and cheerier.
So grab some fabric, your iron, and your creativity. You might just find L-O-V-E!

Materials

Yardages are based on 42"-wide fabric.

⅝ yard of cherry print for borders and appliqués

½ yard of red checked fabric for borders and appliqués

¼ yard *total* of assorted light yellow fabrics for backgrounds

¼ yard of bright red fabric for inner border and appliqués

5" x 9" piece of red fabric for appliqués

⅜ yard of dark red fabric for binding

⅞ yard of fabric for backing

25" x 33" piece of batting

⅜ yard of lightweight fusible web

Red embroidery floss

Cutting

All measurements include ¼"-wide seam allowances.

From the assorted light yellow fabrics, cut a total of:

8 squares, 4½" x 4½"

From the bright red fabric, cut:

2 strips, 1" x 17½"

2 strips, 1" x 8½"

From the red checked fabric, cut:

2 strips, 2" x 42"

3 squares, 5¼" x 5¼"; cut twice diagonally to yield 12 quarter-square triangles

6 squares, 2⅞" x 2⅞"; cut once diagonally to yield 12 half-square triangles

From the cherry print, cut:

3 strips, 2½" x 42"

4 squares, 5¼" x 5¼"; cut twice diagonally to yield 16 quarter-square triangles

2 squares, 2⅞" x 2⅞"; cut once diagonally to yield 4 half-square triangles

Appliqué Blocks

❶ Using the patterns on pages 46 and 47, trace each appliqué shape onto the paper side of the fusible web. Note that the patterns have already been reversed for fusible appliqué. Cut out each shape, leaving about ¼" margin all around the outside of the traced line.

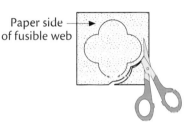

Paper side of fusible web

❷ Following the manufacturer's instructions for the fusible web, and the instructions on each pattern, fuse the shapes to the wrong side of each fabric. Cut out each shape on the drawn line.

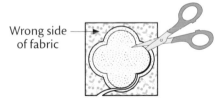

Wrong side of fabric

Cut on the drawn line.

❸ Remove the paper and position a shape in the center of each 4½" yellow square. Fuse the appliqué pieces in place.

❹ Referring to "Embroidery Stitches" on page 75, use two strands of red embroidery floss to blanket stitch around the outside of each appliqué shape. Make eight appliquéd blocks.

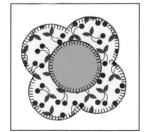

Quilt Top Assembly

1 Sew the appliquéd blocks together in two horizontal rows of four blocks each, alternating letter and picture blocks in each row and from row to row; press. Sew the rows together as shown; press.

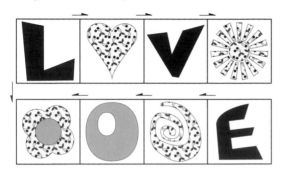

2 Referring to the quilt assembly diagram at right, sew the 1" x 8½" red strips to each shorter side of the L-O-V-E rectangle; press. Sew the 1" x 17½" red strips to the top and bottom of the rectangle.

3 Sew the 2"-wide red checked strips together end to end to make one long strip. Refer to "Borders" on page 76 to measure, cut, and sew the strips to the sides and then the top and bottom of the quilt as shown in the quilt assembly diagram.

4 To make the pieced side borders, sew two 5¼" red checked triangles and three 5¼" cherry print triangles together, offsetting the points as shown; press. Make two. To make the pieced top and bottom borders, sew four 5¼" red check triangles and five 5¼" cherry print triangles together; press. Make two. Sew a 2⅞" red checked triangle to both ends of each border strip; press.

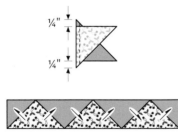

Make 2.

Make 2.

5 Sew each remaining 2⅞" red checked triangle to a 2⅞" cherry print triangle as shown to make a half-square-triangle unit; press. Make four units.

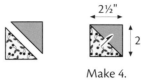

Make 4.

6 Sew a pieced side-border strip to each side of the quilt. Sew a half-square-triangle unit to both ends of each remaining pieced border strip and sew the border strips to the top and bottom of the quilt as shown in the quilt assembly diagram.

7 Sew the cherry print strips together end to end to make one long strip. Refer to "Borders" to measure, cut, and sew the strips to the sides and then the top and bottom of the quilt for the outer border. Press the seam allowance toward the outer border.

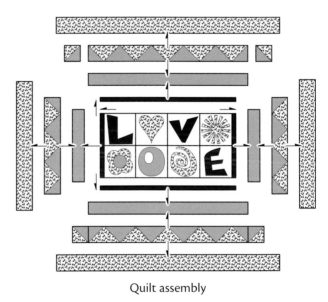

Quilt assembly

Finishing the Quilt

1 Referring to "Finishing the Quilt" on page 77, prepare the backing fabric, and then layer the backing, batting, and quilt top; baste. After basting the layers together, hand or machine quilt as desired. (If you are taking your quilt to a long-arm quilter, you don't need to baste the layers together.)

2 Referring to "Binding" on page 78, cut and prepare approximately 110" of 2¼"-wide bias binding. Sew the binding to the quilt.

QUILTING SUGGESTION

I machine quilted around each appliqué design and quilted a swirl motif in the background.
Then I quilted a large swirl in the triangle border and wavy lines in the outer border.

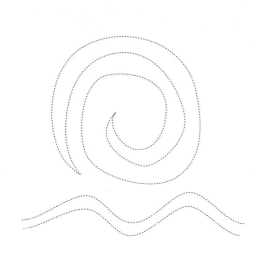

Patterns are reversed
for fusible appliqué.

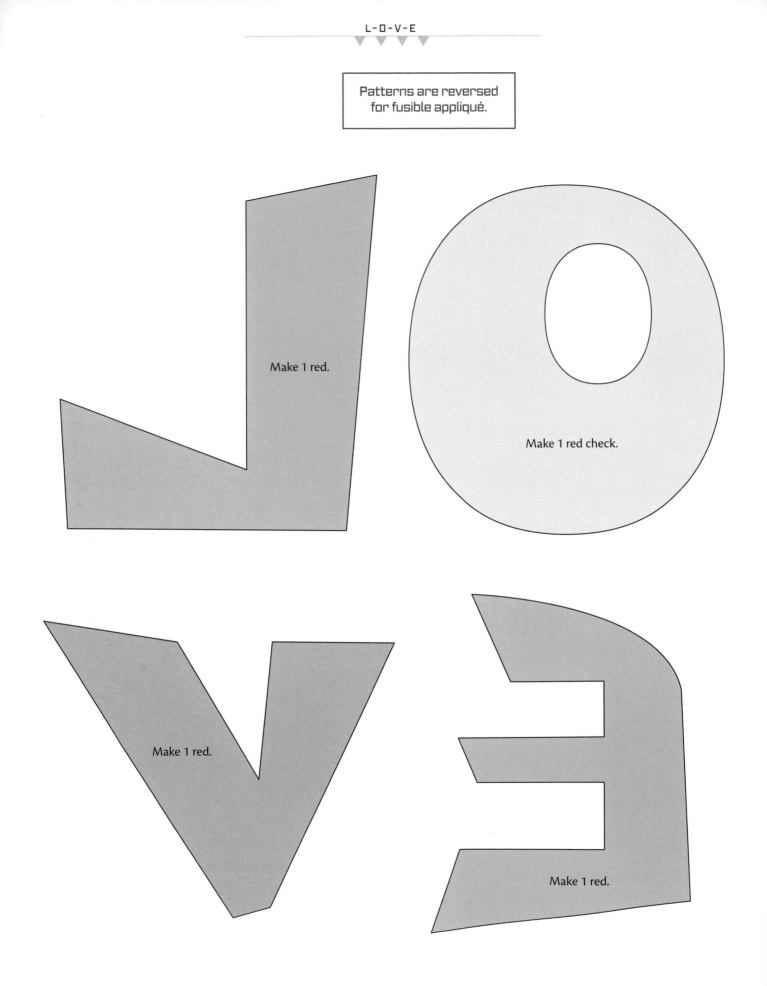

Make 1 red.

Make 1 red check.

Make 1 red.

Make 1 red.

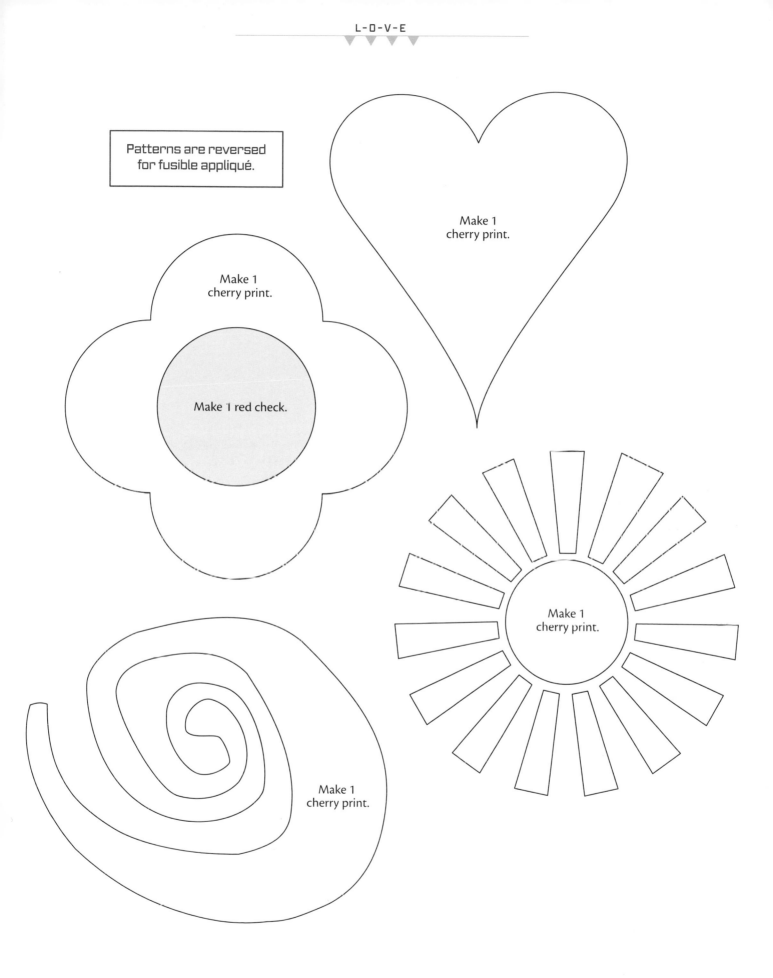

Patterns are reversed
for fusible appliqué.

Make 1
cherry print.

Make 1
cherry print.

Make 1 red check.

Make 1
cherry print.

Make 1
cherry print.

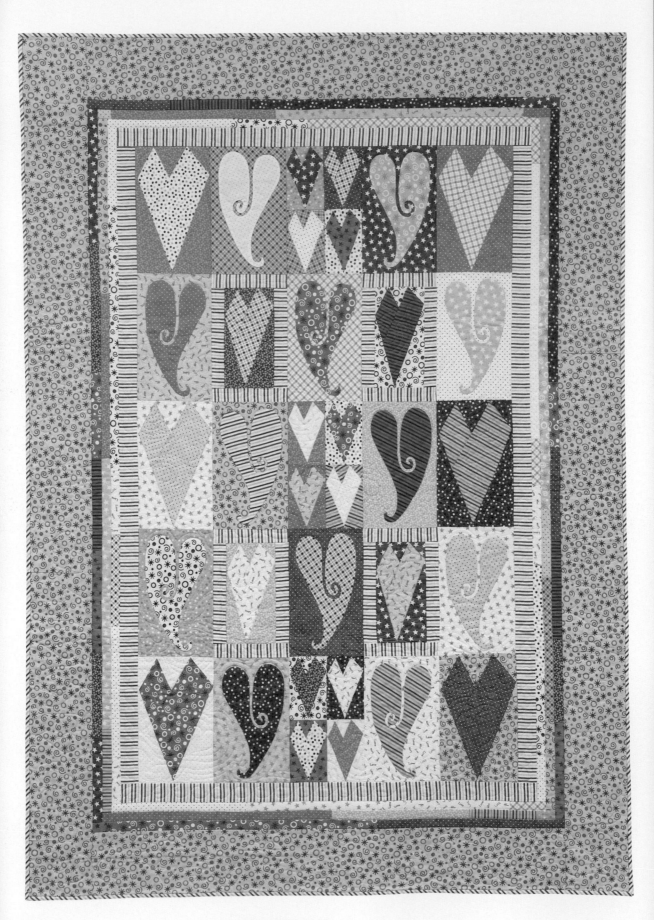

Finished Quilt: 48" x 68"
Finished Blocks: 6" x 10"

HAVE A HEART

Pink hearts—I can't think of a better way to show support for breast cancer awareness. We love our sisters who have fought this disease, and pray for the success of all women who suffer in its grasp. Think pink! Quilt pink!

Materials

Yardages are based on 42"-wide fabric. Fat quarters measure 18" x 21".

1¼ yards of medium pink print for blocks and outer border

1 yard of pink striped fabric for blocks, inner border, and binding

5 to 6 fat quarters *each* of assorted light, medium, and dark pink fabrics for blocks (15 to 18 fat quarters total)

3¼ yards of fabric for backing

52" x 72" piece of batting

Freezer paper

Cutting

All measurements include ¼"-wide seam allowances.

From the assorted pink fat quarters, cut a *total* of:

11 rectangles, 6½" x 10½"

From the light pink fat quarters, cut a *total* of:

9 strips, 1¼" x 21"

From the medium pink fat quarters, cut a *total* of:

10 strips, 1¼" x 21"

From the dark pink fat quarters, cut a *total* of:

10 strips, 1¼" x 21"

From the medium pink print, cut:

6 strips, 5½" x 42"

1 rectangle, 6½" x 10½"

From the pink striped fabric, cut:

5 strips, 2" x 42"

8 strips, 1½" x 8½"

8 strips, 1½" x 6½"

Appliquéd Heart Blocks

For each block you'll use a 6½" x 10½" pink rectangle for the background and a contrasting pink fabric for the heart appliqué. Refer to the photo on page 48 for color-placement ideas.

❶ Referring to "Appliqué" on page 73 and using the heart pattern on page 55, trace the appliqué shape onto the dull side of the freezer paper and cut out the template. Make the quantity specified on the pattern.

❷ Press each freezer-paper template onto the right side of the selected heart fabric and trace. The traced line will be your stitching line. Cut out each appliqué shape, leaving a scant ¼" seam allowance around the marked lines. Peel the freezer paper off of the fabric.

❸ Position each heart shape in the middle of a background rectangle, and hand appliqué in place. Make 12 appliquéd Heart blocks, 6 regular and 6 reversed.

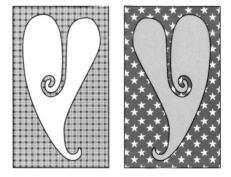

Make 6 and 6 reversed.

Large Heart Blocks

These blocks are paper pieced; refer to "Paper Piecing" on page 75 for details as needed. For each block, choose a background fabric and a contrasting heart fabric.

❶ Enlarge the large heart foundation pattern on page 54 and make six copies.

❷ From the chosen background fabric, cut a strip 4½" x 21". From the chosen heart fabric, cut a strip 4" x 21". Refer to the "Helpful Hint" below for guidance on cutting the fabric shapes.

HELPFUL HINT

When making paper-pieced blocks, I like to precut large pattern pieces so that I can save fabric. I trace the pattern onto the dull side of freezer paper, and then, using a rotary cutter, I cut the pattern into individual pieces on what would be the stitching line.

I then lightly press the various freezer-paper templates shiny side down onto the *wrong side* of the fabric strip and cut each piece leaving a generous ½" seam allowance on all sides of the template. Then I peel the freezer paper off of the fabric.

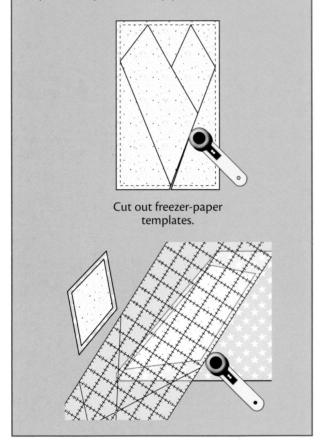

Cut out freezer-paper templates.

---

❸ Stitch the fabrics to the foundation using the heart fabric for pieces 1 and 3, and the background fabric for pieces 2, 4, 5, 6, and 7.

❹ Trim the blocks to 6½" x 10½". Remove the foundation paper.

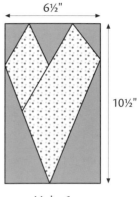

Make 6.

Medium Heart Blocks

These blocks are paper pieced; refer to "Paper Piecing" on page 75 for details as needed. For each block, choose a background fabric and a contrasting heart fabric.

❶ Enlarge the medium heart foundation pattern on page 53 and make four copies.

❷ From the chosen background fabric, cut a strip 3½" x 21". From the chosen heart fabric, cut a strip 3" x 21". Cut out the fabric shapes as described in "Helpful Hints". Peel the freezer paper off of the fabric.

❸ Stitch the fabrics to the foundation using the heart fabric for pieces 1 and 3 and the background fabric for pieces 2, 4, 5, 6, and 7. Use the 1½"-wide strips of pink striped fabric for pieces 8, 9, 10, and 11.

❹ Trim the blocks to 6½" x 10½". Remove the foundation paper.

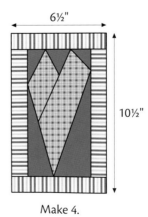

Make 4.

Small Heart Blocks

These blocks are paper pieced; refer to "Paper Piecing" on page 75 for details as needed. For each block, choose four different background fabrics and four different contrasting heart fabrics.

❶ Make 12 copies of the small heart foundation pattern on page 52.

❷ From the chosen background fabric, cut a strip 2½" x 21". From the chosen heart fabric, cut a strip 2" x 21". Cut out the fabric shapes as described in "Helpful Hint" on page 50. Peel the freezer paper off of the fabric.

❸ Stitch the fabrics to the foundation using the heart fabric for pieces 1 and 3 and the background fabric for pieces 2, 4, 5, 6, and 7.

❹ Trim the blocks to 3½" x 5½". Remove the foundation paper.

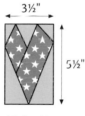

3½"

5½"

Make 12.

❺ Sew four Small Heart blocks together as shown to make a large block. Make three blocks.

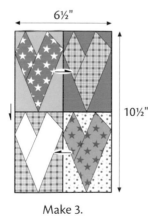

6½"

10½"

Make 3.

Quilt Top Assembly

❶ Arrange the appliquéd Heart blocks and the paper-pieced blocks in five rows of five blocks each as shown in the quilt assembly diagram at right.

❷ Sew the blocks into rows. Press the seam allowances toward the appliquéd blocks. Sew the rows together. Press the seam allowances in one direction.

❸ Sew three of the 2"-wide strips of pink striped fabric together end to end to make one long strip. Refer to "Borders" on page 76 to measure, cut, and sew the strips to the sides of the quilt for the inner border. Using the remaining 2"-wide strips, measure, cut, and sew the strips to the top and bottom of the quilt. Press all seam allowances toward the newly added borders.

❹ Trim the 1¼"-wide light pink strips to random lengths. Sew the light pink strips together end to end to make one long strip, at least 180" long. Measure, cut, and sew the strips to the sides and then the top and bottom of the quilt for the first middle border. Press all seam allowances toward the newly added borders.

❺ Repeating step 4 using the 1¼"-wide medium pink strips, make a 186"-long strip and attach it for the second middle border. Press all seam allowances toward the newly added borders.

❻ Repeating step 4 using the 1¼"-wide dark pink strips, make a 195"-long strip and attach it for the third middle border. Press all seam allowances toward the newly added borders.

❼ Refer to "Borders" to measure, cut, and sew a 5½" wide medium pink strip to the top and bottom of the quilt. Sew two of the remaining medium pink strips together end to end to make a long strip. Make two long strips. Then measure, cut, and sew the strips to the sides of the quilt for the outer border. Press all seam allowances toward the newly added borders.

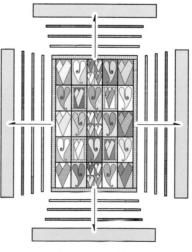

Quilt assembly

Finishing the Quilt

1 Referring to "Finishing the Quilt" on page 77, prepare the backing fabric, and then layer the backing, batting, and quilt top; baste. After basting the layers together, hand or machine quilt as desired. (If you are taking your quilt to a long-arm quilter, you don't need to baste the layers together.)

2 Referring to "Binding" on page 78, cut and prepare approximately 245" of 2¼"-wide bias binding. Sew the binding to the quilt.

QUILTING SUGGESTION

I machine quilted around each appliquéd heart and filled in the background with an echo heart motif. I then quilted in the ditch along the middle borders, half hearts running down the center of the inner border, and quilted a heart motif in the outer border.

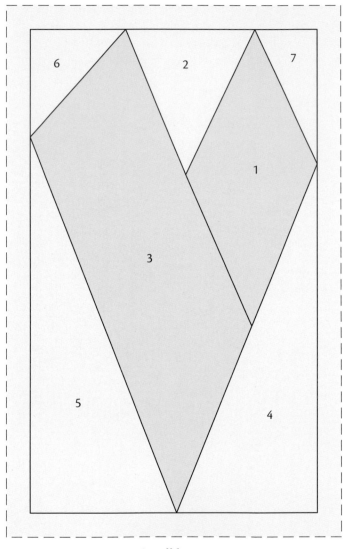

Small heart

Enlarge pattern 125%.

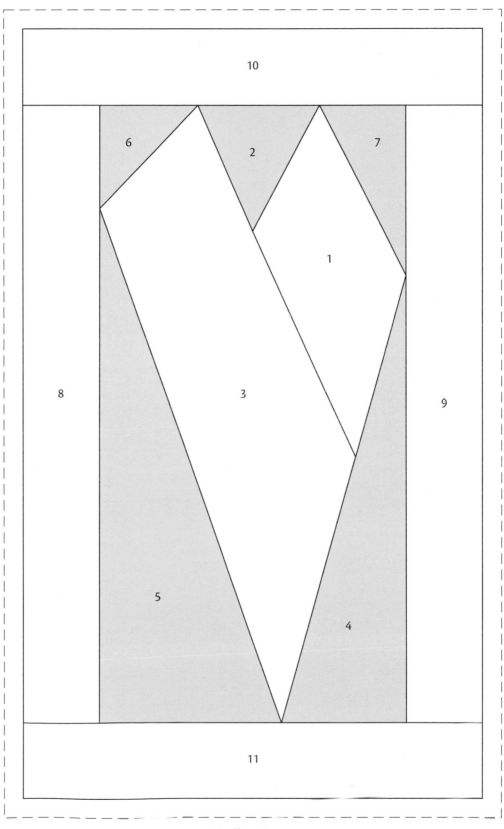

Medium heart

Enlarge pattern 125%.

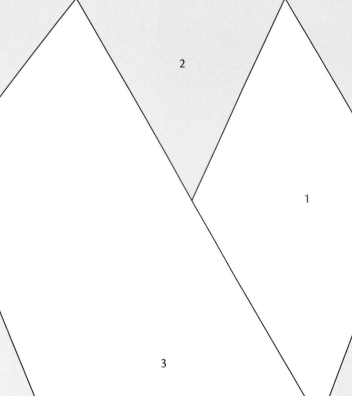

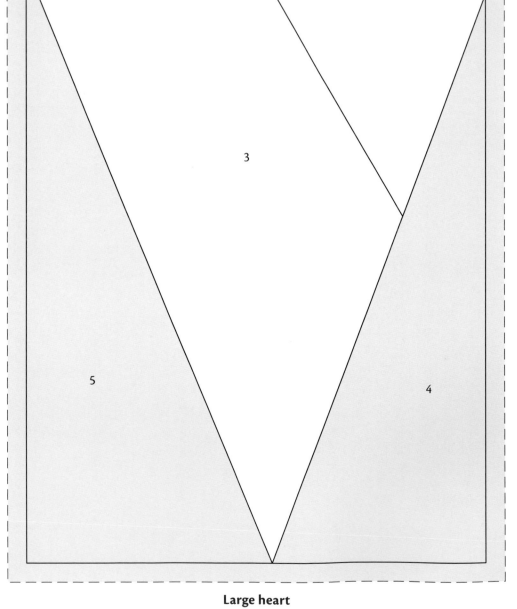

Large heart

Pattern does not include
seam allowance.

Appliqué heart
Make 6 and 6 reversed from light,
medium, and dark pink.

Center

Finished Quilt: 52½" x 72½"
Finished Blocks: 8" x 12"

EVERY BLOOMING THING

Lots of bright colors and flowers—who could ask for anything more?
This quilt just about covers every blooming thing!

Materials

Yardages are based on 42"-wide fabric. Fat quarters measure 18" x 21".

1⅛ yards of white fabric for block backgrounds
1 yard of white dotted print for blocks and outer border
½ yard of bright striped fabric for blocks and inner border
1 fat quarter *each* of 15 assorted bright prints (purple, lime, and teal) for blocks and outer border
Scraps of bright green for appliqués
⅝ yard of purple fabric for binding
3½ yards of fabric for backing
57" x 77" piece of batting
Freezer paper
Template plastic

Cutting

All measurements include ¼"-wide seam allowances.

From the white fabric, cut:
4 strips, 8½" x 42", crosscut into 12 rectangles, 8½" x 12½"
2 rectangles, 2½" x 6½"

From the white dotted print, cut:
5 strips, 5½" x 42"; crosscut 1 *of the strips* into:
    4 squares, 5½" x 5½"
    8 rectangles, 1½" x 5½"
2 rectangles, 2½" x 6½"
2 rectangles, 1½" x 6½"
2 rectangles, 1½" x 4½"

From the fat quarters of 15 assorted bright prints, cut a *total* of:
8 strips, 5½" x 21"
48 rectangles, 2½" x 8½"*
9 rectangles, 2½" x 6½"
22 rectangles, 1½" x 6½"**
22 rectangles, 1½" x 4½"**
*You'll need 4 matching rectangles for each block.
**You'll need 4 matching rectangles (2 of each size) for each block.

From the bright striped fabric, cut:
7 strips, 1½" x 42"; crosscut 1 *of the strips* into:
    2 rectangles, 1½" x 6½"
    2 rectangles, 1½" x 4½"
4 rectangles, 2½" x 8½"

Appliquéd Flower Blocks

❶ Referring to "Appliqué" on page 73 and using the stem, leaves, and flower patterns on pages 61–66, trace the appliqué shapes onto the dull side of the freezer paper and cut out each template.

❷ Using the bright green and the bright prints, press each freezer paper template shiny side down onto the right side of the fabric and trace. The traced line will be your stitching line. Cut out each appliqué shape, leaving a scant ¼" seam allowance around the marked lines. Peel the freezer paper off of the fabric. Refer to the photo on page 56 for color-placement ideas. (Set aside one flower L to appliqué in the outer border.)

❸ Position the stem, leaves, and flower in the middle of each white 8½" x 12½" rectangle, and hand appliqué in place. Appliqué the pieces in numerical order as indicated on each pattern. Make 12 appliquéd Flower blocks, 6 regular and 6 reversed.

Rectangular Blocks

Each block is made from three fabrics, one fabric for the center rectangle, one fabric for the 1½"-wide inner rectangles, and one fabric for the 2½"-wide outer rectangles. Refer to the photo on page 56 for color-placement ideas.

1 Sew a 1½" x 6½" rectangle to each long side of a 2½" x 6½" rectangle; press. Sew a 1½" x 4½" rectangle from the same fabric as that used for the outer sides to the top and bottom as shown; press.

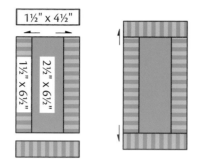

2 Using four 2½" x 8½" rectangles from the same fabric, sew a rectangle to each side of the unit; press. Then sew a rectangle to the top and bottom of the block; press. Make 13 blocks.

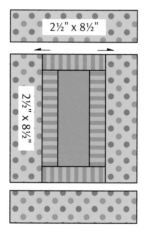

Make 13.

Triangle Border

Patterns for pieces A and B appear on page 60.

1 Referring to "Rotary Cutting Template Shapes" on page 72, make plastic templates for pieces A and B. From the 5½"-wide white dotted strips, cut 40 pieces using template A and your rotary-cutting tools. From the assorted bright strips, cut 36 pieces using template A, four pieces using template B, and four pieces using template B reversed.

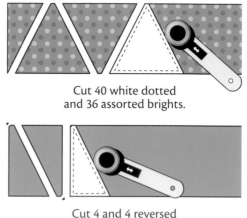

Cut 40 white dotted and 36 assorted brights.

Cut 4 and 4 reversed assorted brights.

2 To make the pieced top and bottom borders, sew eight white dotted A pieces, seven bright A pieces, and two bright B pieces (one regular and one reversed) together, offsetting the points as shown; press. Sew a 1½" x 5½" white dotted rectangle, to each end of the border strip. Make two.

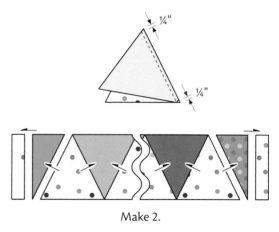

Make 2.

3 To make the side borders, sew 12 white dotted A pieces, 11 bright A pieces, and 2 bright B pieces (one regular and one reversed) together, offsetting the points; press. Sew a 1½" x 5½" white dotted rectangle to each end of the border strip; press. Then sew a 5½" white dotted square to both ends of each strip; press. Make two.

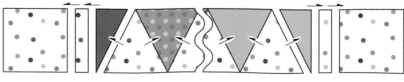

Make 2.

Quilt Top Assembly

1 Arrange the blocks in five rows of five blocks each, alternating the Flower blocks and the Rectangular blocks in each row and from row to row as shown in the quilt assembly diagram below.

2 Sew the blocks in each row together; press the seam allowances toward the Rectangular blocks. Sew the rows together; press the seam allowances in one direction.

3 Sew the bright striped strips together end to end to make one long strip. Refer to "Borders" on page 76 to measure, cut, and sew the strips to the top and bottom, and then the sides of the quilt for the inner border. Press the seam allowances toward the newly added borders. The quilt should measure 42½" x 62½".

4 Sew a short triangle border strip to the top and bottom of the quilt; press toward the narrow border. Sew a long triangle border strip to each side of the quilt for the outer border; press.

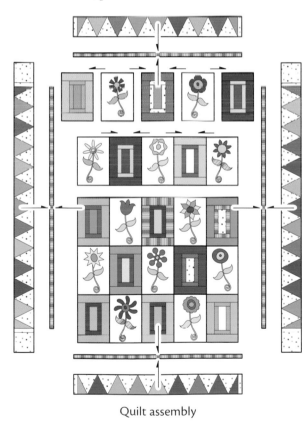

Quilt assembly

5 Hand appliqué the prepared flower L from step 2 of "Appliquéd Blocks" to the upper-left corner of the outer border as shown in the photo on page 56.

Finishing the Quilt

1 Referring to "Finishing the Quilt" on page 77, prepare the backing fabric, and then layer the backing, batting, and quilt top; baste. After basting the layers together, hand or machine quilt as desired. (If you are taking your quilt to a long-arm quilter, you don't need to baste the layers together.)

2 Referring to "Binding" on page 78, cut and prepare approximately 260" of 2¼"-wide bias binding. Sew the binding to the quilt.

QUILTING SUGGESTION

I machine quilted around each appliquéd flower design and filled in the background with a meandering design. I used the flower designs to quilt a flower motif in each rectangular block and then echo quilted the motif. In the border, I quilted a continuous-line design with a swirl flower and leaves.

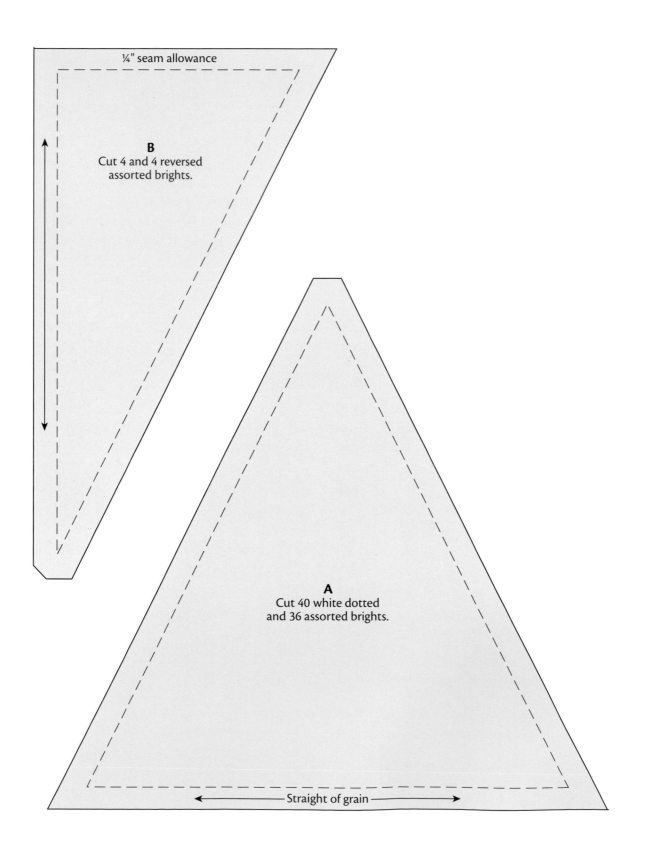

¼" seam allowance

B
Cut 4 and 4 reversed
assorted brights.

A
Cut 40 white dotted
and 36 assorted brights.

Straight of grain

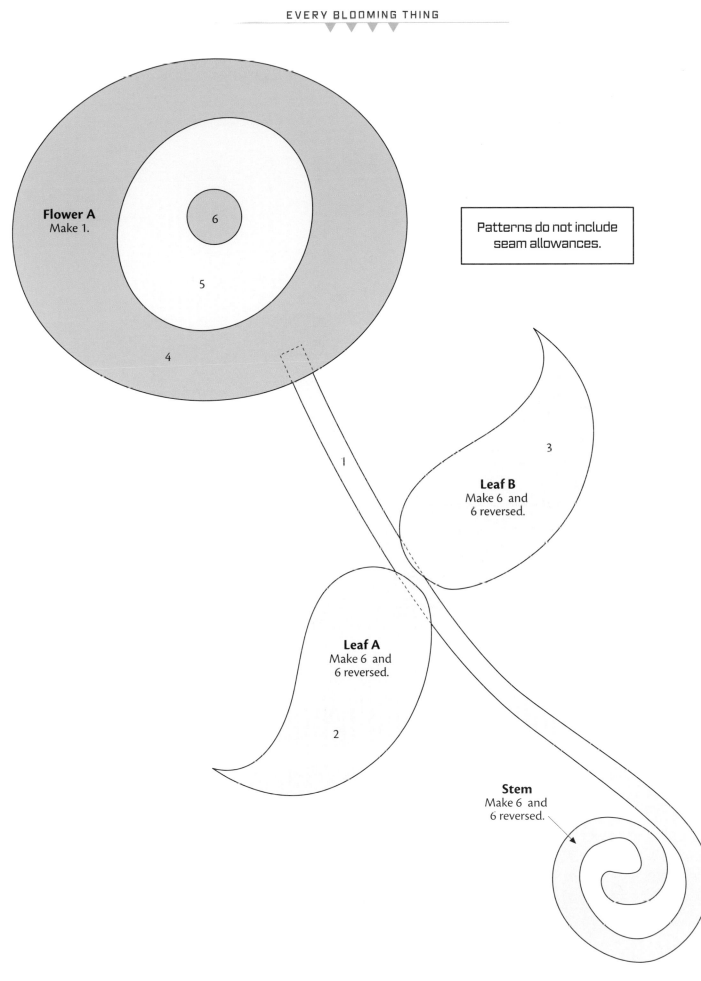

Flower A
Make 1.

6

5

4

Patterns do not include
seam allowances.

1

3

Leaf B
Make 6 and
6 reversed.

Leaf A
Make 6 and
6 reversed.

2

Stem
Make 6 and
6 reversed.

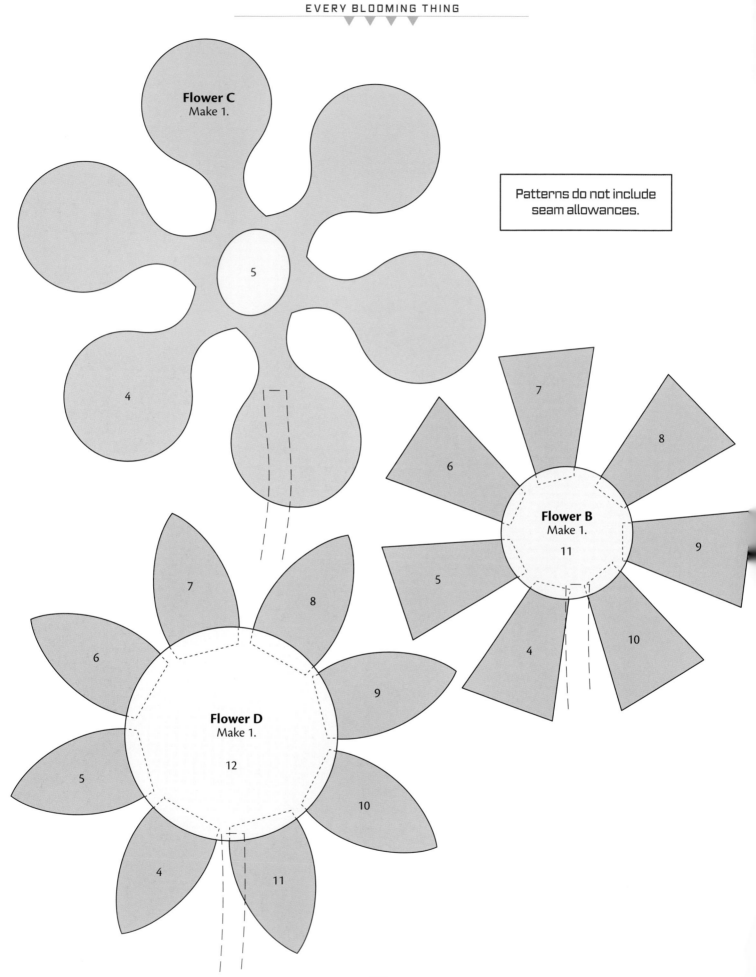

Flower C
Make 1.

Patterns do not include
seam allowances.

Flower B
Make 1.

Flower D
Make 1.

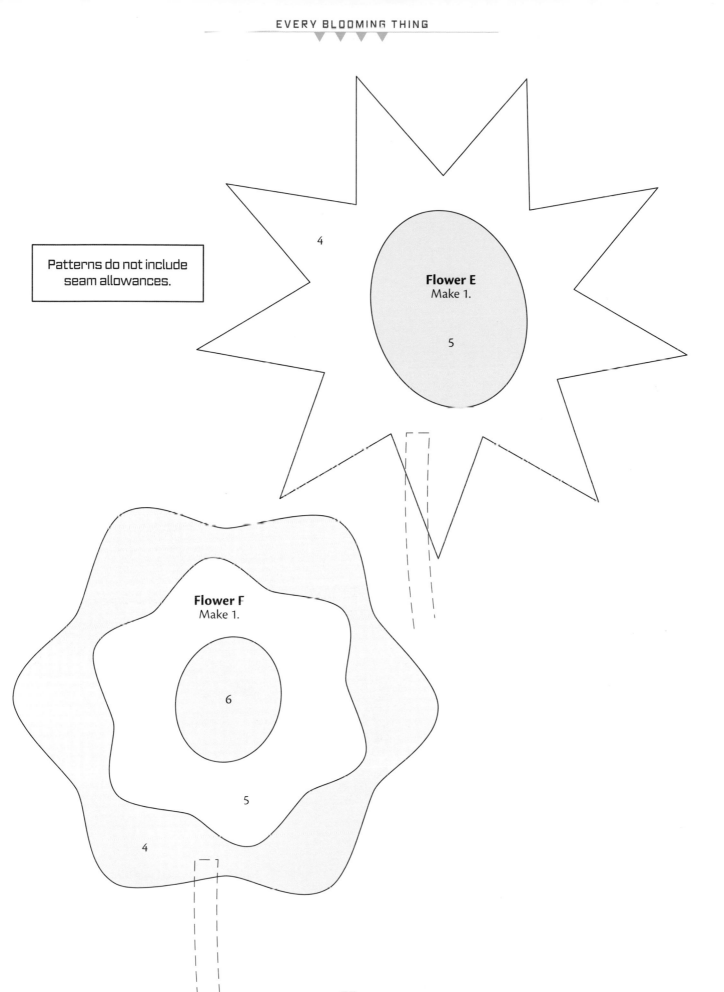

Patterns do not include
seam allowances.

Flower E
Make 1.

4

5

Flower F
Make 1.

6

5

4

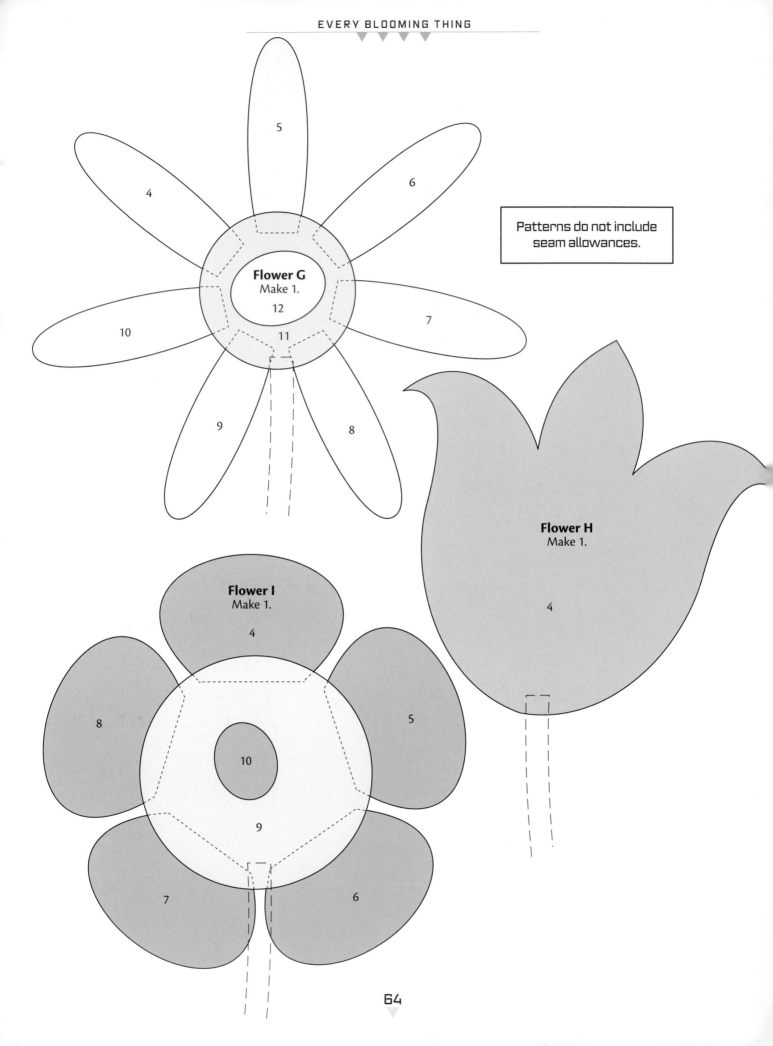

Patterns do not include
seam allowances.

Flower G
Make 1.

5
4
6
10
7
12
11
9
8

Flower H
Make 1.

4

Flower I
Make 1.

4
8
5
10
9
7
6

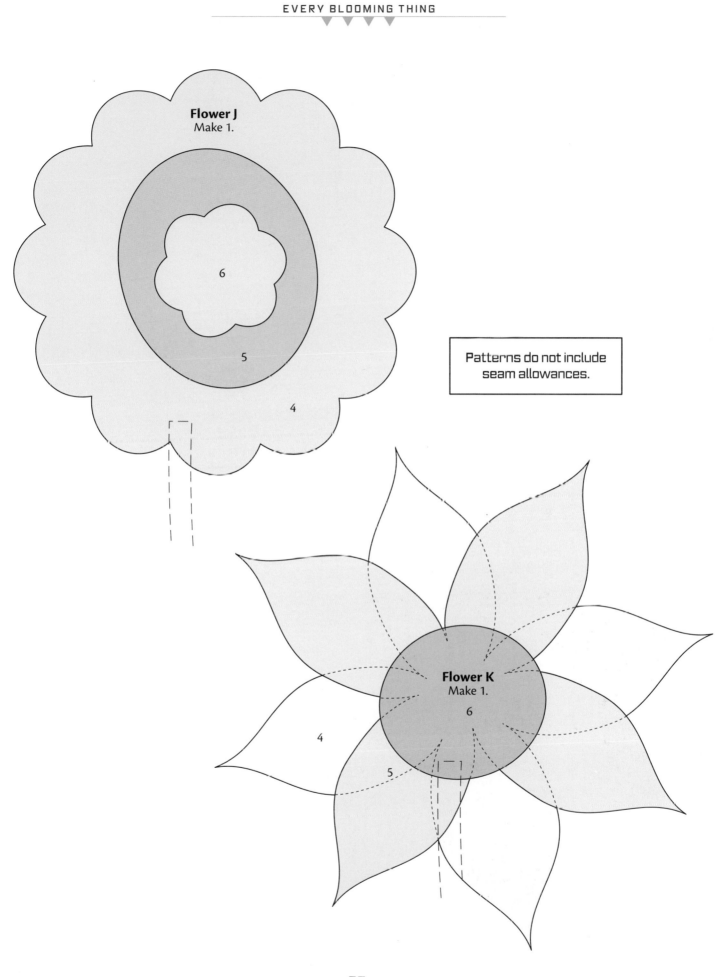

Flower J
Make 1.

6

5

4

Patterns do not include
seam allowances.

Flower K
Make 1.

6

4

5

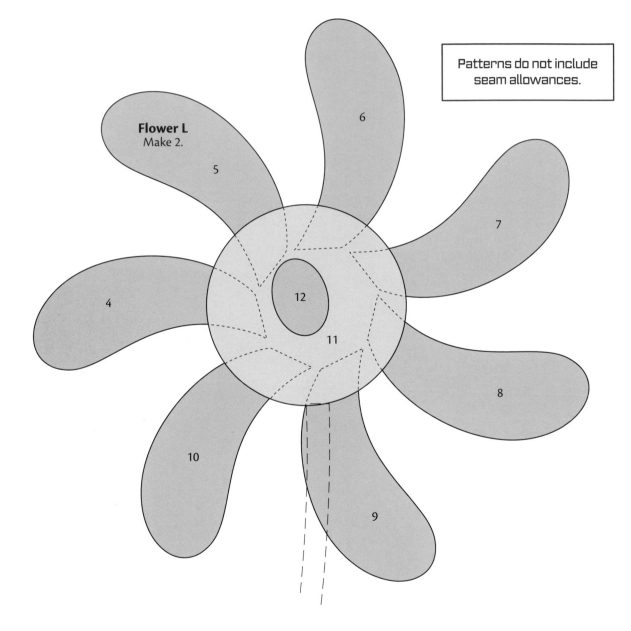

Flower L
Make 2.

Patterns do not include seam allowances.

4

5

6

7

8

9

10

11

12

FRUIT BASKET

Finished Quilt: 59¼" x 84¾"
Finished Blocks: 12" x 12"

FRUIT BASKET

Fruit basket tipped over—I loved this game as a kid! When I saw the fruit fabric, I knew it needed a fun and easy quilt pattern. Use fruit fabric, or any other great focus fabric, and let *it* spill all over the place, too!

Materials

Yardages are based on 42"-wide fabric. Fat quarters measure 18" x 21".

1⅔ yards of bright fruit fabric for block centers and outer borders

⅞ yard of bright green fabric for sashing

⅝ yard of bright pink fabric for blocks

⅝ yard of bright orange fabric for blocks

1 fat quarter *each* of 12 assorted bright prints (yellow, pink, red, and green) for blocks

⅝ yard of orange striped fabric for binding

5½ yards of fabric for backing

64" x 89" piece of batting

Cutting

All measurements include ¼"-wide seam allowances.

From the bright fruit fabric, cut:
4 strips, 6½" x 42"; crosscut into 24 squares, 6½" x 6½"
7 strips, 4" x 42"

From the fat quarters of 12 assorted bright prints, cut a *total* of:
120 strips, 1½" x 21"

From the bright pink fabric, cut:
5 strips, 3½" x 42"; crosscut into 48 squares, 3½" x 3½"

From the bright orange fabric, cut:
5 strips, 3½" x 42"; crosscut into 48 squares, 3½" x 3½"

From the bright green fabric, cut:
20 strips, 1¼" x 42"; crosscut *10 of the strips* into 28 strips, 1¼" x 12½"

Block Assembly

❶ Randomly sew together six 1½"-wide assorted bright strips along their long edges to make a strip set; press. Make 20. Crosscut the strip sets into 96 segments, 3½" wide.

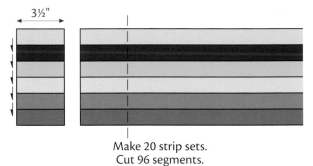

Make 20 strip sets.
Cut 96 segments.

❷ Sew a segment from step 1 to each side of a 6½" square as shown to make a center unit; press. Make 24 center units.

Make 24.

❸ Sew a pink square to each end of a segment from step 1 as shown to make 24 pink units; press. Sew an orange square to each end of a segment from step 1 to make 24 orange units; press.

Make 24.

Make 24.

4 Sew a pink unit to the top and bottom of 12 of the center units from step 2 as shown; press. Make 12 pink blocks.

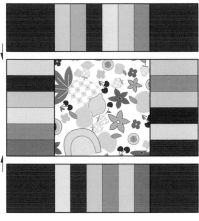

Pink block.
Make 12.

5 Sew an orange unit to the top and bottom of each remaining center unit as shown; press. Make 12 orange blocks.

Orange block.
Make 12.

Quilt Top Assembly

1 Arrange seven 1¼" x 12½" green sashing strips, three pink blocks and three orange blocks, alternating the blocks as shown. Sew the blocks and sashing strips together to make a row; press. Make four rows.

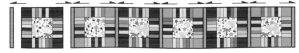

Make 4.

2 Measure the length of each of the four block rows. If they differ, calculate the average and consider this the length. Sew two 1¼"-wide green strips together end to end to make a long sashing strip. Make five. Trim each long strip to the correct length.

3 Referring to the "Helpful Hint" box on page 40, sew the block rows and the five long sashing strips together, alternating them as shown in the quilt assembly diagram. Press the seam allowances toward the sashing strips.

4 Sew the 4"-wide fruit print strips together end to end to make one long strip. Refer to "Borders" on page 76 to measure, cut, and sew the strips to the sides and then the top and bottom of the quilt for the outer border.

Quilt assembly

Finishing the Quilt

1 Referring to "Finishing the Quilt" on page 77, prepare the backing fabric and then layer the backing, batting, and quilt top; baste. After basting the layers together, hand or machine quilt as desired. (If you are taking your quilt to a long-arm quilter, you don't need to baste the layers together.)

❷ Referring to "Binding" on page 78, cut and prepare approximately 300" of 2¼"-wide bias binding. Sew the binding to the quilt.

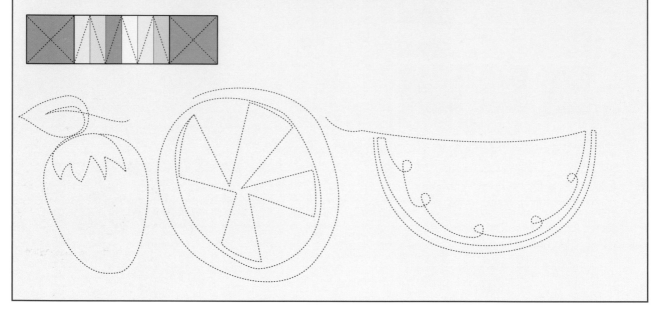

QUILTING SUGGESTION

I machine quilted diagonal lines over the small rectangles and cross lines in the corner squares of each block. Then I quilted a different fruit in the center of each block, and repeated the fruit motifs in the border.

QUILTMAKING BASICS

The quiltmaking techniques used in this book are some of my favorites. There are many different methods for each aspect of quilting, and it's important to find the methods that work best for you. Accuracy in cutting and sewing yields the best results. All of the yardage requirements in this book are based on 42"-wide fabrics that provide at least 40" of usable fabric after prewashing.

Fabric Selection

The best results will be achieved by using 100%-cotton fabric for your quilts. If you purchase your fabric from a quilt shop, it will be good quality fabric that will wear well. You don't want to spend time making a quilt that will fall apart after the first washing because it was made with inferior fabric. Color selection is one of my favorite aspects of making a quilt, but I know this can be stressful for some people. Enjoy the process, and make each quilt your own. The staff at most quilt stores will be happy to assist you in selecting fabrics if you need help.

Rotary Cutting

Using the proper tools is an important component of making your quilts as accurately as possible. A good rotary cutter and cutting mat are indispensable. Always keep your rotary blade sharp; a sharp blade will make it easier to cut pieces accurately. Another necessary tool is a good ruler. My favorite is a 6" x 24" acrylic ruler. There are many great rulers and tools available to make quilting easier, but you'll be able to make all of the projects in this book with this ruler. Although, I also find a square ruler is useful for crosscutting squares from strips. Square rulers come in many different sizes, but I like a larger one (9½" or larger) for squaring up blocks and finished quilts. Always use the measurements on the ruler, not the ones on the mat. I've found rulers to be more accurate than the lines on a mat.

To cut strips, fold the fabric so that the selvages meet. Lay the fabric on the cutting mat with the folded edge toward you. Fold the fabric again toward the selvage. Place the ruler on top of the fabric along the right edge, aligning your rotary ruler with the fabric fold. The raw, uneven edges should extend beyond the ruler's edge. Cut along the long edge of the ruler to trim off the end

of fabric, making a straight edge. Discard this strip. (Reverse this procedure if you are left-handed.)

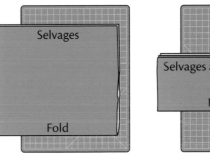
Fabric folded once

Fabric folded twice

Turn the fabric or mat around and place the straightened edge to your left. Cut strips in the width specified in the project instructions, measuring from the straight edge. For example, if you need a 2"-wide strip, place the 2" line of the ruler on the straightened edge of the fabric and cut along the right edge of the ruler.

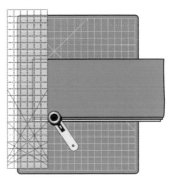

To cut squares and/or rectangles from a strip, unfold the cut strip once so that it is folded in half. Place the selvage edges to your right and make a cut, creating straightened edges as you did previously. Place the newly cut edges to your left. Align the proper measurement on your ruler with the straightened end of the strip and cut the fabric into squares or rectangles.

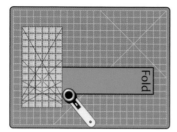

To make half-square triangles, cut the squares once diagonally from corner to corner. To make quarter-square triangles, cut the squares twice diagonally from corner to corner.

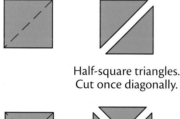

Half-square triangles.
Cut once diagonally.

Quarter-square triangles.
Cut twice diagonally.

ROTARY CUTTING TEMPLATE SHAPES

Some of the quilts in this book require you to use a template to cut a triangle shape. To make a template, trace the pattern provided onto template plastic with a fine-tipped permanent-ink pen. Use utility scissors to cut out the template. Place the template back over the pattern in the book and check to make certain you have cut it accurately. If the template has trimmed triangle tips, you can trim them from the template at this time. Place the template on the fabric strip as directed in the project instructions. *Carefully* cut around each shape with a rotary cutter.

Piecing

The most important aspect of quiltmaking is to maintain an accurate ¼" seam allowance. This ensures that all of the seams will match and the various pieces will fit together properly. Using a ¼" presser foot on your machine will give you the best results, but if your machine doesn't have one, you can create a seam guide by placing a piece of masking tape ¼" from the needle. Place a ruler under the presser foot and lower the needle onto the ¼" mark. Mark the seam allowance by placing a piece of masking tape at the edge of the ruler. Be careful not to cover the feed dogs on your sewing machine.

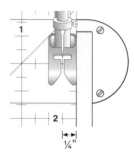

When sewing several identical fabric pieces together, I like to chain piece them to save time and reduce the amount of thread used. To chain piece, sew the first pair of pieces together. At the end of the seam line, stop sewing but do not cut the thread. Feed the next pair of pieces under the pressure foot and continue sewing in the same manner until all the pieces are sewn. Remove the chain of pieces from the machine and clip the threads between the pairs as you press them.

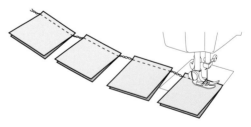

Pressing

Pressing is an important detail when making your quilts. Your quilt top will lie much flatter if you carefully press your work after stitching each seam. Be sure to use an up-and-down motion, rather than the gliding motion of ironing, to avoid stretching the fabric. Pressing directions are provided with each project. In general, it is common to press seam allowances toward the darker fabric or toward the section with fewer seams.

Appliqué

There are many different appliqué methods, but the method I prefer is needle-turn appliqué. All the projects in this book use needle-turn appliqué except "L-O-V-E," which uses fusible appliqué. Fusible appliqué instructions are included with the project.

In this section, you'll find some basic needle-turn appliqué instructions, but remember there are many books available for learning more about appliqué techniques.

Marking the Appliqué Pieces

I use freezer-paper templates to make the appliqué shapes. In addition, you can use a freezer-paper template several times before it will no longer stick to your fabric.

❶ Place the freezer paper, shiny side down, over the design, and trace the design onto the dull side with a fine-lead mechanical pencil. Do not reverse the image, unless instructed otherwise.

❷ Cut out the template on the traced lines so that they are the exact size of the pattern pieces.

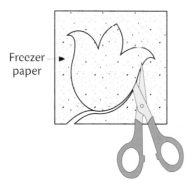

Freezer paper

❸ Place the freezer-paper template with the shiny (coated) side facing the right side of the appliqué fabric. Leave at least ½" between pieces. Press the template to the right side of the fabric using a hot, dry iron. Let the piece cool.

Right side of fabric

½"

❹ Draw a line around the templates with a mechanical pencil. For dark fabrics, I use a yellow or white lead pencil, kept sharp. This line will be your stitching line. Remove the freezer-paper template.

❺ Cut out the fabric appliqué piece leaving a scant ¼" seam allowance around the marked line.

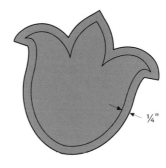

¼"

Appliqué Placement

An easy way to place the appliqué pieces on the background blocks is to use a light table. Once you've traced or copied the pattern from the book, place it on the light table, and lay your background block over it. Position the appliqués on the block, overlapping where indicated and paying careful attention to the stitching order marked on the pattern. Use appliqué glue to secure the pieces in place, usually one small drop in a few key places is enough. (Or if you prefer, pin each piece in place using appliqué pins.)

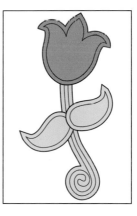

If you find it difficult to see the pattern from the book through a medium or dark background fabric, try a pattern overlay. With a contrasting-color permanent pen, trace the pattern onto a piece of cellophane or clear acetate that is the same size as your background fabric. Place the plastic over the background fabric, pinning it in place if desired. To position each appliqué piece, lift up the plastic and slide each piece under the appropriate marking. Remove the plastic overlay, and then glue or pin the appliqué pieces to the background fabric.

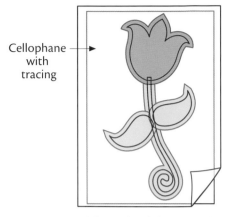

Cellophane with tracing →

Slide appliqué shapes under the overlay to place them on the background.

Hand Appliqué Stitch

The traditional appliqué stitch is the same for all hand appliqué methods. Stitches should be small and even. Use a single strand of thread in a color that closely matches the appliqué. Tie a knot in one end. If you are right-handed, hold the fabric with your left thumb on top and your middle finger on the bottom directly under the appliqué. You'll be stitching from right to left. (Reverse this procedure if you are left-handed.)

Turn under a small section of the seam allowance with your needle and finger-press. Slip your needle into the seam allowance from the wrong side of the appliqué piece (not the background fabric), bringing it out through the folded edge of the appliqué. Make the first stitch into the background fabric, directly below where the needle emerged. Bring the needle up again about 1/8" away, through the background fabric and catching one or two threads on the folded edge of the appliqué.

Continue to take small, even stitches, turning the seam allowance under with the tip of the needle as you go and catching just the folded edge with each stitch. Be sure to turn under enough seam allowance to cover your drawn lines. Continue stitching a couple of stitches past where you began. Knot the thread on the wrong side of the background fabric. When all the appliqué is complete, gently press the block.

Below are four basic elements that will help you to achieve a quality needle-turn appliqué stitch: The inside curve, the outside curve, the inside point, and the outside point all require different techniques.

For an inside curve, clip almost to the line to ease the fabric around the curve smoothly. Before making your stitch, sweep around the curve with your needle, turning the seam allowance under.

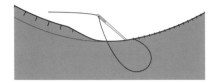

For an outside curve, ease the fabric around the curve pushing the seam allowance under with the tip of your needle and smoothing the folded edge before sewing. Keeping your stitches a bit smaller will help create a smoother curve.

For an inside point, as you stitch toward an inside point, stop stitching before you get to the inside point and clip right to the line, at the point. Use your needle to sweep the seam allowance under. Stitch to the clip, and take one or two stitches right at the clip; then turn, sweep the seam allowance under, and continue to sew.

For an outside point, stitch on the first side of the piece very close to the point. Take one extra stitch, very close to the first stitch. This extra stitch will hold the fabric securely as you turn the point. Flip the point under; then sweep the seam allowance under on the next side and continue to sew.

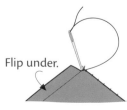

Flip under.

Embroidery Stitches

I used four basic stitches for the embroidery in this book. Unless indicated otherwise, I use two strands of embroidery floss.

Straight Stitch

The straight stitch is used for straight lines or to outline a shape.

Knot the end of your floss. Bring your needle up at A, go down at B, and come up at C. Repeat this pattern along an entire line. Knot your thread at the back.

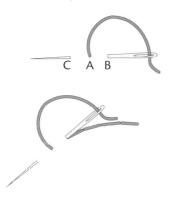

French Knot

French knots can be used for making small dots.

Knot the end of your floss. Bring your needle up at A. Wrap the floss around the needle two or three times, keeping the thread taut. Reinsert the needle back down at B, very close to A. Hold the wrapped thread right next to the fabric as you pull the thread through to the back of your work. Pull the thread through completely, leaving the knot next to the fabric on the top. You can make several French knots close together, and then knot your thread at the back.

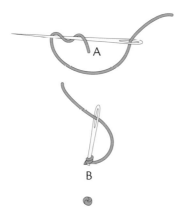

Satin Stitch

I use a satin stitch to fill in areas, such as the eyes on the sheep on "Counting Sheep."

Knot the end of your floss. Bring the needle up at point A and go down at point B. Bring it up again at point C, and continue stitching until the area is filled in.

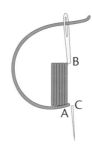

Blanket Stitch

The blanket stitch makes a great decorative element around the appliquéd edge.

Knot the end of your floss. Starting at the edge of the appliqué motif, bring the needle up at A. Insert the needle at B and reemerge at C. Keep the thread below your work and underneath the needle when it emerges at C. Pull the thread through to form a loop that lies under the emerging thread. The loop should lie snuggly against the fabric without pulling or distorting it.

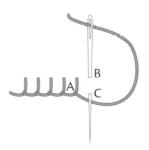

Paper Piecing

Paper piecing is a great way to get accurate seams when sewing odd angles or sharp points.

Make as many photocopies of the paper foundation pattern as you will need. To ensure accuracy, be sure to make all copies for your quilt project on the same copy machine. Select paper that you can see through easily, holds up while sewing, and is easy to remove afterward. A lightweight paper made specifically for foundation piecing or vellum are good choices. You can also trace the pattern onto foundation papers if you prefer. The marked lines are your sewing lines. All fabric is placed on the blank (unmarked) side of the foundation pattern. Fabric pieces are sewn to the foundation paper in numerical order.

1 Cut your fabric as specified in the project instructions.

2 Place the first fabric piece on the unmarked side of the foundation paper, right side up. Hold the fabric and foundation paper up to the light to make sure that area 1 is completely covered, plus an ample seam allowance.

3 Place fabric piece 2 on top of fabric piece 1, right sides together. Hold the pieces up to the light to make sure that there is at least ¼" of fabric extending over the line that separates areas 1 and 2.

4 Set your sewing-machine stitch length between 15 and 20 stitches per inch. Holding the layers firmly in place, turn the foundation over, and carefully position the unit under the presser foot, paper side up. Sew on the line between areas 1 and 2, starting about ¼" before the line and extending ¼" beyond.

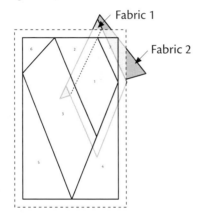

Fabric 1

Fabric 2

5 Trim seam allowances to ¼" wide, being careful not to cut the foundation paper. Flip open piece 2 and press the fabric into place with a dry iron.

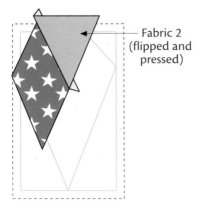

Fabric 2
(flipped and pressed)

6 Continue sewing the pieces to the foundation paper in numerical order until the block is complete.

7 Trim away the excess fabric around the edges of the block, being sure to leave a ¼" seam allowance. Remove the foundation paper, and press the block.

Borders

The borders must be cut to fit the center measurement of the quilt. If you cut them without measuring the quilt through the center, the borders might not fit properly and your quilt will end up looking wavy or puckered.

The fabric requirements for the borders in this book are based on cutting the border strips on the crosswise grain, unless otherwise indicated. Cut strips the width indicated in the cutting instructions for your quilt. If the quilt is larger that the length of one strip, you will need to sew the strips together end to end with a straight or diagonal seam, and then cut strips the exact length from the longer strip. I generally prefer to sew the top and bottom borders to the quilt first, and then sew the side borders. However, for some of the quilts I stitched the side borders first, and then added the top and bottom borders so that I could cut fewer strips.

1 Measure the width of your quilt from side to side through the center. Cut two border strips to this length, piecing as necessary.

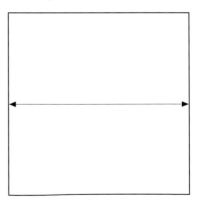

2 Fold each border strip in half to find the center, and then fold the strip again to divide it into four parts. Mark the folds with pins as shown. Mark the quilt in the same manner. Pin the borders to the top and bottom edges of the quilt, matching the pins and ends. Ease or slightly stretch the quilt to fit the border strip as necessary. Sew the top and bottom borders in place with a ¼"-wide seam allowance and press the seam allowances toward the borders.

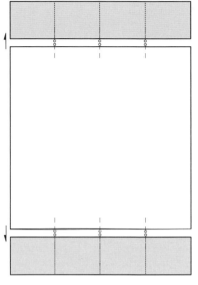

Pin-mark.

❸ Measure the length of the pieced top through the center, including the just-added borders. Cut two border pieces to this measurement, piecing as necessary. Fold each border strip in half to find the center, and then fold the strip again to divide it into four parts. Mark the folds with pins as shown. Mark the quilt-top in the same manner. Pin the borders to the sides of the quilt, matching the pins and ends. Sew the side borders in place with a ¼"-wide seam allowance, easing as necessary, and press the seam allowances toward the borders.

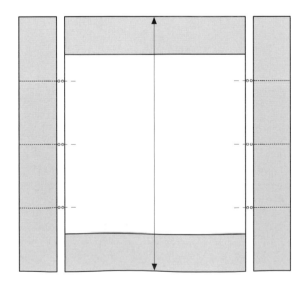

Finishing the Quilt

Your quilt top is now complete and you need to decide how you will quilt it. If the design needs to be marked on the quilt, marking should be done before layering the quilt with the backing and batting.

Backing

For the quilt backing you should use a high quality 100%-cotton fabric. Your quilt back should be at least 4" larger than the quilt top (2" to 3" on all sides). If your quilt is larger than the standard width of fabric, you will need to stitch two or more pieces of fabric together to make the backing. You can place the seams anywhere you want. Remove the selvages before sewing the pieces together. Press the seam allowances open to make quilting the top easier.

Long-Arm Quilting

If you plan to take your quilt to a professional long-arm quilter, check with the quilter before preparing your finished quilt top and backing. In general, the quilt back should be at least 2" to 3" larger on all sides for putting the quilt on the machine. Most long-arm quilters will have batting you can purchase, or you can provide your own batting. I prefer 100%-cotton batting, but some 80%-cotton/20%-polyester battings work well too. For long-arm quilting, thick batting isn't a good choice because it's difficult for the machine to quilt through.

Layering and Basting

You can choose to quilt your project by hand or machine. Whichever method you choose to use, the quilt top, batting, and backing will need to be layered and basted together.

❶ Press the backing fabric and quilt top. Mark the center of the quilt top and backing on all four sides.

❷ Spread the backing, wrong side up, on a clean, flat surface. Use masking tape to anchor the backing to the surface without stretching the fabric.

❸ Center the batting over the backing, smoothing out any wrinkles and making sure it covers the entire backing.

❹ Center the pressed top, right side up, on the batting and backing. Align borders and straight lines of the quilt top with the edges of the backing, smoothing any wrinkles from the center out.

77

5 For hand quilting, baste with needle and thread starting in the center of the quilt; baste a grid of horizontal and vertical lines 6" to 8" apart. For machine quilting, you may baste the layers with #2 rustproof curved safety pins. Place the safety pins about 6" to 8" apart, away from the areas you intend to quilt, and remove the pins as you go.

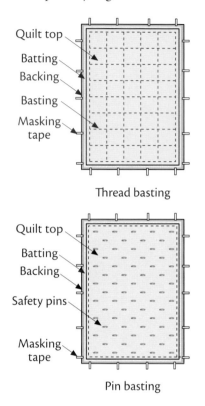

Quilt top
Batting
Backing
Basting
Masking tape

Thread basting

Quilt top
Batting
Backing
Safety pins
Masking tape

Pin basting

Binding

My favorite quilt binding is a double-fold binding made from bias strips. The two layers of fabric resist wear, and the bias has some give so it rolls over the edges of the quilt nicely. I think it simply looks better on a completed quilt.

After quilting, trim excess batting and backing even with the edge of the quilt top.

1 To make bias-binding strips, trim the selvage from one edge of the fabric with your rotary cutter and ruler.

2 Fold one corner of the fabric diagonally as shown. Align your ruler so that the 45° mark is parallel with the cut edge, and the long edge of the ruler is just inside the folded diagonal edge as shown. Trim off the fold.

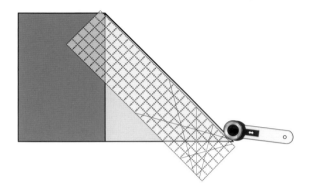

3 Remove the large triangle and set side. Align your ruler along the diagonally cut edge to cut bias strips to your desired width (I make mine 2¼").

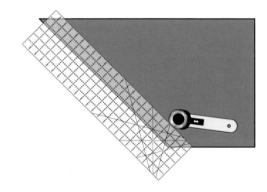

4 Sew bias strips together offsetting them as shown. Press the seam allowances to one side.

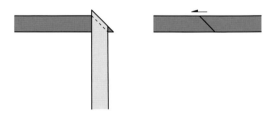

5 Press the strip in half lengthwise, wrong sides together and with raw edges aligned.

6 Starting near the middle of one side, align the raw edges of the folded binding with the edge of the quilt-top front. Leave a 5" to 6" tail of binding free. Using a ¼"-wide seam allowance, sew the binding in place. Stop ¼" from the corner of the quilt, sew at a 45° angle to the edge of the quilt as shown.

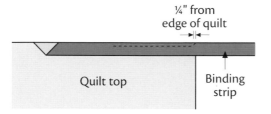

¼" from edge of quilt

Quilt top

Binding strip

7 Remove the quilt from the sewing machine. Miter the corner by folding the binding straight up and, away from the quilt, making a 45° angle along the fold. Fold the binding back down onto itself, even with the edge of the quilt top to create an angled pleat at the corner. Begin with a backstitch at the fold of the binding and continue stitching along the edge of the quilt top.

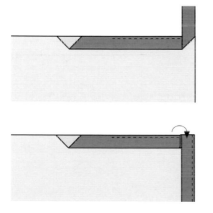

8 Continue around the quilt in the same manner, mitering each corner as you come to it. Stop sewing about 6" to 7" from where you started, and backstitch. Remove the quilt from the machine. Unfold the binding and overlap the beginning tail with the end, and then mark a diagonal line on the end tail even with the edge of the beginning tail. Make a second mark ½" to the right of the first mark. Cut the binding end at a 45° angle, cutting on the second mark.

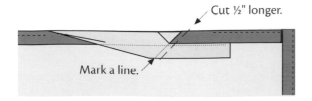

Cut ½" longer.

Mark a line.

9 Sew the two ends right sides together; press. Refold the binding in half and press. Finish sewing the binding in place.

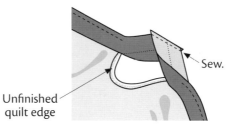

Unfinished quilt edge

Sew.

10 Turn the binding to the back of the quilt. Using thread to match the binding, hand stitch the binding in place so that the folded edge covers the row of machine stitching. At each corner, fold the binding to form a miter on the back of the quilt.

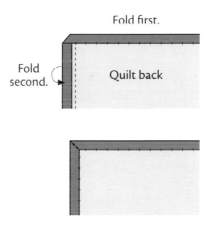

Fold first.

Fold second.

Quilt back

ABOUT THE AUTHOR

Cheryl Brown started out as a commercial interior designer, where she enjoyed working with color, texture, and fabric. She shifted gears into the quilting world a few years later, when she became a stay-at-home mom and took up quilting as a hobby. She has been quilting for many years now, and it never grows old!

She works for a quilt store, where she also teaches classes, and she is a long-arm quilter. She started her own business, Elephant Patch, two years ago, when she also started designing quilts. This is her first book.

Cheryl lives in Centerville, Utah, with her husband, Neil, her two children, Adrian and Natalie, and her wacky cat, Daisy.